Praise for Carol P. Christ's Stunning Memoir

"Like Sappho, the great poet of Aphrodite, (Carol) Christ, agonizing over whether she will ever again experience love, 'has words with' her Goddess. The Goddess grants her a healing vision, and Christ ends the book in a new flowering of self-confidence and self-love." Patricia Monaghan, *Choice*

"In this 'narrative thealogy,' (Carol) Christ shares the spiritual lessons she learns as she seeks to understand her relation to the ground of all Being. Her quest with the Goddess begins out of a jarring sense of loss and abandonment caused by the death of her mother and leads her to an exhilarating experience of healing and rebirth. Her journey confirms for her as well the relational and embodied character women's experience of the divine. Luminous prose." *Booklist*

"In her lyrical and intensely honest book Carol Christ communicates both the joy of new vision and the pain that gives it birth. The brilliant and courageous author of such feminist classics as *Diving Deep and Surfacing* and *Laughter of Aphrodite* felt she could no longer trust herself, her deepest feelings and intuitions, the Goddess . . . or life itself. Then during a trip to the mountaintop shrines and sacred caves of Crete, she gradually discovered her own inner strength and eventually learned that she is not alone." Christine Downing, author of *The Goddess* and *Women's Mysteries*

D0920621

"(Carol) Christ writes with great courage and honesty." Starhawk, author of *The Spiral Dance* and *City of Refuge*

"Many artists and writers have journeyed through Greece to re-connect with deep and mysterious sources of creativity and joy. Recently Carol Christ, a well-known feminist author and theologian, discovered for herself the transformative powers of the Cretan landscape. In *A Serpentine Path*, she reveals what Greece has taught her as she leads a group of North American women on a healing pilgrimage to the sites and shrines where female divinity was worshipped. Her profoundly spiritual story will be an inspiration to people who long to remember, renew, and reinvent ancient forms of Goddess rituals and magic." Naomi Goldenberg, author of *The Changing of the Gods*

"In *A Serpentine Path*, Carol Christ recreates the wonderful healing journey she leads in Crete for women reclaiming their connection to the sacred feminine. As we ascend with her to mountaintop shrines and climb deep into sacred caves she helps us re-connect with the spirit of the ancient pre-patriarchal Goddess that is a living entity in this fertile land and culture. Christ invites the reader into the deeply revealing story of her own spiritual awakening and we, too, are transformed." Maureen Murdock, author of *The Heroine's Journey*

"This book changed my life." Gina Messina-Dysert, Founder of The FAR Press and co-founder of *Feminism and Religion*.

"An evocative celebration of Cretan—and female—power."
– *Kirkus Reviews*

A Serpentine Path

Neolithic Goddess from Crete, c. 5550 BCE

A Serpentine Path

Mysteries of the Goddess

Carol P. Christ

(fp)

The FAR Press
An imprint of Blaise Publications
Cleveland, Ohio
www.thefarpress.com

Copyright © 2016 by The FAR Press

All rights reserved.

No part of this book may be reproduced or distributed in any format including print and electronic without permission.

A Serpentine Path is a revised version of a book published as *Odyssey with the Goddess* in 1995 by Continuum Publishing Company; all rights reverted to the author.

Cover art "Downward Serpent" by Judith Shaw. Frontispiece photo taken in the Heraklion Archaeological Museum by Mika Scott. Permission to reprint Sappho's poetry from *Sappho: A New Translation* (Berkeley, California: University of California Press, 1958), by Mary Barnard, granted by the University of California Press.

ISBN: 978-1-4575-4596-2

This book is printed on acid-free paper.

Printed in the United States of America

This book is dedicated

to

sisters on the journey

and

friends in Crete

Table of Contents

Part Three: *Pilgrimage*

Part Four: *Rebirth*

Two steps left
Two steps right
Into the darkness
Into the light

Preface

A *Serpentine Path* is a story that begins in despair and ends in rebirth and regeneration. It depicts a turning point in my life, a psychological and spiritual breakthrough that opened me to living the rest of my life in grace and joy. Though I am tempted to say it was a journey from darkness to light, that would be inaccurate, for mine was a journey into the darkness and out again. The path of life is never straight or narrow, and the circle of light and darkness is never-ending.

When I began the journey described in *A Serpentine Path*, I did not feel loved, I did not want to live, I could not write, and I believed the Goddess had betrayed my faith. As I completed the book, I knew I was loved, I wanted to live, I was writing, and I understood that the Goddess had never abandoned me. Though my life has had its ups and downs since then—as all lives do—I have never forgotten that I am loved, I have wanted to live, I have not stopped writing, and I feel the Goddess ever-present in my body, in my breath, and in my connections with the living and the dead. Though my story is deeply personal, my struggles with love and death, trust and control, are widely shared.

A story of finding the Goddess, *A Serpentine Path* is part of a growing genre[1] that is developing as women explain to themselves and others why they left the patriarchal religions of their origins for a more nourishing spiritual vision that affirms both women and the earth. *A Serpentine Path* documents the first of the Goddess Pilgrimages to Crete I have been leading twice a year since then.[2] For the women who have traveled with me, it will evoke many memories. For those who have dreamed of a pilgrimage to the Goddess, it offers an opportunity to imagine the journey. I now know a great deal more about ancient Crete, the folklore and customs of traditional Crete, and the rocks, trees and plants of Crete, than I did when I began. *But I learned the mystery on my first pilgrimage.* Because we are all deeply connected to each other, I know that the path to the mystery I discovered is not mine alone.

This book is a narrative thealogy[3] in which the Goddess is revealed, and the nature of divinity unfolds in a story. In graduate school I discovered theology to be an abstract discourse disconnected from the questions of meaning and value that arise in our lives. My career as a scholar, teacher, and writer has been defined by a search to find ways to connect theology and experience: from my early study of the poetry of the Hebrew Bible; to my dissertation on Elie Wiesel's stories; to my first book, *Diving Deep and Surfacing,* on spiritual quest in women's literature; to *Laughter of Aphrodite,* where I struggled to unite the first person voice of experience with the third person objective voice of the scholar.[4]

In *A Serpentine Path* I find my own voice and write about divinity in the world from the standpoint of my own experience: it marks a turning point in my writing. When I completed this book, I was prepared to undertake the daunting task of writing the first contemporary Goddess thealogy, *Rebirth of the Goddess.* There, and in my next book, *She Who Changes,* I explored the theological and philosophical meanings of the Goddess, writing from the standpoint of the experiences I had described in *A Serpentine Path.* In our jointly-written book, *Goddess and God in the World,* Judith Plaskow and I model an "embodied theological method," exploring the complex inter-relation of autobiography and theology, as we discuss our different views of divinity. Readers who wonder about how my life and thinking developed after *A Serpentine Path* will want to continue on to the books that followed.[5]

A Serpentine Path was originally published as *Odyssey with the Goddess,* a title chosen by and insisted upon by the publisher. I never felt comfortable with it, because the

Odyssey of Homer was named after the warrior Odysseus, and I did not envision myself as a modern-day male hero. The book had an unlucky fate. Despite having received positive and even glowing initial reviews, it was withdrawn from print after a negative review in a feminist publication. The reviewer stated that no feminist worth her salt would allow her heart to be broken by a man; and not being particularly spiritual herself, she was mystified by the rest of the story. Had I been asked to respond at the time, I would have agreed with her that feminism teaches us not give our power over to men. But, I would have added, women have been harmed on bodily, emotional, and spiritual, as well as intellectual levels by patriarchy. *There is often a gap between what we know in our minds and what we feel in our hearts and in our bodies. It was precisely this disconnect and the healing of body, mind, and spirit that I addressed in my book.*

I am grateful to sister feminist theologian Melissa Raphael for telling me that *Odyssey with the Goddess* was her favorite of all my books, a confidence I have treasured over the years; and to Betty Bequart Sanders, Elizabeth Chloe Erdmann, Mika Scott, Laura Shannon, and Christa Schoeniger for urging me to republish it. Members of the spring 2015 Goddess Pilgrimage to Crete asked me to make all of my books available in e-book format and this prompted Betty to suggest that it would not be difficult to retype *Odyssey with the Goddess,* as it is a short book. This sparked me to imagine republishing *Odyssey with the Goddess* using its original more evocative title. Retyping the manuscript myself, I omitted details that in retrospect seemed unnecessary and refined the prose, but did not change the story, or add anything other than the Preface and the Epilogue. As I worked on the first two parts of the book, I felt I was polishing a stone, so that it would shine more brightly. When I came to the section on the pilgrimage, another metaphor seemed appropriate: I was cutting loose threads while reweaving the central threads of the narrative: the intertwined stories of the pilgrimage and my pilgrimage. I made almost no changes in part four.

Christine Downing broke my writing block when she asked me to write about my mother's dying. Pat Felch heard many of the stories in this book as I began to write them. Marie Canton and Frank Oveis were thoughtful editors of the original manuscript.

Carol P. Christ,
Mithymna, Lesbos, Greece, late summer 2015

Part One

UNDERWORLD

I poured a libation to all the dead,
first with milk and honey,
and then with sweet wine,
then with water.[6]

In Aphrodite's Island

*Last night
I dreamed that
you and I had
words, Cyprian.[7]*

ore than two and a half thousand years ago, the poet Sappho was bold enough to express her anger at the Goddess Aphrodite. I too had been having words with Her. Or more precisely, holding onto an enormous anger that precluded words. I no longer prayed to the Goddess who had inspired me to hope that eros and ecstasy could be mine. I no longer trusted my deepest feelings and intuitions, the source not only of my relationship to the Goddess, but also of my creativity. It had become a struggle for me just to live, to suppress the words that came unbidden into my mind, threatening to blot out all else: *"No one understands me, no one loves me, no one will ever love me, I might as well die."* I believed I had a right to be angry with the Goddess because my devotion to Her had brought me to live in Her island and, in a deeper sense to the impasse where I found myself.

I had first come to Greece, reluctantly, ten years earlier. My friend Ellen, who had fallen in love with Greece, organized a summer institute in Lesbos and insisted I teach a course on Greek Goddesses. Though I had been seeking the Goddess for many years, the Greek Goddesses were not in my blood. I was not one of those girls whose mothers read them bedtime stories of Greek Goddesses, nor had I learned about them in school. In college, my passion had been for the Hebrew Bible, and it was natural that I was drawn to the Hebrew Goddesses. Astarte naked holding flowers and Asherah with a body like the trunk of a tree moved me more than Athena, born from the head of Zeus or Hera, the betrayed wife. Because I understood the Goddess to be embodied in nature, I felt called to learn about the Grandmothers of the American land where I lived. But Ellen would not take no for an answer, and so, in the late spring, I packed my bags and travelled to Lesbos, to teach the Greek Goddesses. I did not know then that one summer would become five, or that in time, I would choose to live in Greece.

Lesbos is a large island with pine forests in the mountains. Eleven million silver green olive trees dot the hillsides. The land embraces the wide Gulf of Kalloni, "the Beautiful," in its center. Mithymna, the village where we stayed, is built on a volcanic hill at the island's northernmost end, in sight of the shores of Turkey. Achilles is said to have plundered Mithymna during the Trojan War. Grey stone houses with gaily colored shutters and terra cotta roofs climb the sides of a hill topped by an austere fortress built by Genoese warlords on much older foundations. It was last occupied by the Turks who lost control of the island in 1912, and were forced to leave following the defeat of the Greek army in Asia Minor in 1922. Turkish words are part of village dialects.

Lesbos was home to Sappho, Greece's most honored lyric poet, whom Plato called "the tenth muse." The muses still sing in Lesbos, in the tinkling of sheep's bells and in the plaintive calls of the doves. A local story says that the dove was once a young girl who lost her love. Repeating *deka-okto, deka-okto, he was only eighteen, he was only eighteen,* she turned into the dove whose song commemorates her loss.

The deep bay of Mithymna is sheltered by the hills of Petra on one side, and a tiny fishing harbor on the other. Its waters are placid, and ever-moving currents change its colors from grey to blue to indigo. The crystal clear light unique to Greece is often pierced by the graceful swoops and dives of swallows and house martins that make their mud nests on the sides of the houses. One can swim out a long, long way, all the while looking up at the village, without reaching the open sea. At sunset the black silhouettes of fishing boats crisscross the horizon as the evening star rises in the wake of the setting sun.

Though the Goddess is present in the landscape of Lesbos, there are no impressive ruins of ancient temples. In a place called Mesa, a few grey stones and broken columns in a marshy place where the sea meets the dry land mark the site of a Hellenistic temple to Aphrodite.[8] When women from the institute first visited the site, we found it unfenced, with two trees growing in its center and a spring gurgling nearby. Local farmers and their animals moved slowly in the summer heat. We poured water from a ceramic pitcher into the welcoming earth, and read to each other from the poems of Sappho. It was not difficult to imagine that Sappho and her students had also visited this sacred place.

The next summer Alexis, who was to become a dear friend, and I made a pilgrimage to the temple together, to heal the pain of broken love. As we crossed the threshold of the temple, an unexpected golden laughter filled the air. The laughter of Aphrodite seemed to be telling me not to take my suffering so seriously. Sitting alone between the trees, I felt the warm sun transform the pain in my body. I knew I was being claimed by the Goddess, but I had no inkling that this initiation was the first step on a serpentine path that would lead me to leave behind home and family, work and friends, and move to a foreign land.

The Goddess who claimed me that day was not the superficial Goddess of love, beauty, and sexuality portrayed by Homer and Hesiod. Like all of the Goddesses, Aphrodite

rose from the earth: love and beauty are great gifts of bounteous earth. To be claimed by Aphrodite is to acknowledge
that we too are rooted in the earth. In the ensuing years, I
taught about Aphrodite, wrote about Her, tended Her
shrines, poured libations to Her, and brought women and
girls to be initiated at Her temple. I called myself Her priestess; others said I embodied Aphrodite for them. Swimming
in the grey blue sea of Mithymna, I felt whole, alive, and at
peace with the world.

When I returned to California each fall, I tried to infuse
the energy I felt in Lesbos into my teaching and my daily life.
But with freeway driving bringing me to school, many students taking my courses only to fulfill requirements, ugly
classrooms, bells marking the beginning and ending of our
time together, deadlines and grading, and an institutional
structure that favored objective tests over real learning, I
would begin to feel exhausted and depleted half way
through the fall semester.

Aphrodite was a muse for my writing, inspiring me to
move beyond the objective third person voice of traditional
scholarship into a more poetic, rhythmic, and grounded
style of writing. The story of my initiation as a priestess of
Aphrodite written for a panel at the American Academy of
Religion forced me to bring together two strands in my writing that had previously been separated: my experience of the
Goddess and my theoretical work. In my first book, *Diving*

Deep and Surfacing, on the relation of women's stories to women's spiritual quest, I analyzed stories told by other women. Now I was beginning to write my own narrative thealogy, in which the meaning of the Goddess emerged in the story of my life: I was discovering my authentic voice.

As I came in touch with my deepest feelings and began to express them in my writing, my work deviated further from the accepted academic models. As the Goddess became more and more central in my work, I also began to feel less at home in the Women and Religion section of the American Academy of Religion, which I had helped to found. Those of us who were writing about the Goddess were increasingly censored by a moralistic chorus of Christian feminists who often excluded women who had left the church from their conversations with each other.

In the summers, when I returned to Lesbos, I felt free, and the Goddess seemed to be calling me. In time, as I allowed Aphrodite's power to penetrate my blood and bones, it became more and more difficult to return to a culture that sapped the life energy I felt so strongly in Greece. When my marriage suddenly ended, I took leaves of absence from my job, first for four months, then for a year, then for another. Walking the cobbled steps to my house at the top of Mithymna's hill, looking down across tiled roofs to the sea below, I knew I had come home. In the end, I resigned the tenured full professorship I had worked so hard to achieve.

When I moved to Lesbos, I was warmly greeted by the Greek friends I had made over the years, especially by Axiothea, Ellie, and Nena. Axiothea was the first married woman to open her own business in Mithymna; her mother Ellie began to call herself a feminist as soon as she learned the word; and Nena remembered the summer when Ellen's group first came to Lesbos as the happiest time of her life. Whenever I knocked on their doors, they stopped what they were doing and made Greek coffee for us to share. We communicated in broken Greek and English, and often one of them read our fortunes in the coffee cups.

By lucky chance another American woman, Jude, an artist with a seven year-old son, had come to live in Mithymna the same year. We shared the struggles of adapting to a foreign culture, and talked about how the beauty of the land inspired our best work. Over ouzo and wine, we imagined living all of our lives in Lesbos, comforted each other when we felt lonely, and spoke of our dreams of meeting men with whom we could share the joy that was taking root in our bodies and our souls. In the spring, we travelled together to Aphrodite's temple, where we offered flowers, honey, and wine on an altar we created, pouring out the pain and longing in our hearts, repeating the words Jude spoke first. *"If there is anyone in the universe for me, send him to me or me to him."*

Disappointment

A few days later, I met Andreas,[9] a soulful, intelligent, younger man with an engaging smile and an infectious laugh. He said he wanted to become a writer. He was a passionate and persistent lover, and after a few weeks, he told me that he was in love with me. Adding to that, there was the rose gold sea at sunset, the summer heat, the singing of birds, and my own desire. I allowed myself to believe that the Goddess had sent him to me in answer to my prayers. Watching the stars emerge in the veil of night while sitting on a rock overlooking the sea, we imagined a life together writing, traveling, and endlessly making love.

Those dreams were not to be, and when our relationship ended, the voice of my despair returned: *"No one loves you. No one will ever love you. You might as well die."* The betrayal I felt was not only his betrayal. I felt betrayed by the Goddess who, I believed, sent him to me. I also felt betrayed by my deepest intuitions, which had seemed to confirm that this man and I belonged together. I did not understand why he left me, and I wondered if there was something deeply wrong with me that made me deeply and finally unlovable.

In desperation, I threw myself into another relationship. While it lasted, I was able to hold back the voice inside me. But when it ended too, all the anger, hurt, and confusion returned. *"See,"* the voice said, *"I was right. No one understands you. No one will ever love you."* Thoughts of suicide had plagued me for many years, surfacing when my love affairs came to an end. Always something stopped me. My mother, my friends, the little dog who licked my tears away, my work. This time I was afraid I really might kill myself. I had moved to Athens where I knew almost no one, my little dog had died, my mother was far away, my work seemed meaningless. I had no daily routines to keep me going. And the Goddess seemed to have abandoned me.

As I struggled with my despair, I often felt that there were two of me: the brave, tall, beautiful, blonde, successful, strong, competent feminist with a Ph.D. from Yale and two well-received books on women's spirituality; and inside a desperate creature who only wanted to die. Afraid of that creature's power to annihilate me, I felt the only way to survive was to refuse to listen to her, to kill her if necessary, before she killed me. I struggled to push her voice from my mind, falling asleep with the television on, holding onto a lucky stone to protect me, keeping busy so I would never be alone with my thoughts. Underneath, I was terrified. To the world, for the most part, I presented a calm exterior.

I did survive. I adopted a white calico cat and named her Chloe, the Greek word for the green growth that comes with the fall rains. Chloe was painfully small and afraid. Gradually she gained weight and began to sit on my lap. I started to make new friends. I bought an apartment and threw myself into renovating and furnishing it. I fell in love with two pink, green, and indigo Persian carpets. I ordered a living room set in pink and royal blue velvet. I sewed lace curtains patterned with doves on a friend's machine. I taught myself to hammer and nail, to use a drill, and to make electrical connections. I painted and refinished antique furniture found while shopping with friends in the junk stores of Athens. Physical labor was healing, and I created a beautiful home. I planted a garden in pots on my balcony. Soon it was in bloom. I started having dinner parties, and for the first time in my life found time to enjoy cooking.

My mother shared my enthusiasm for my apartment, and she and my father decided to visit me in Greece. Knowing that Mom was coming, I redoubled my efforts to refurbish my apartment. I said to myself: "Mom will like this; Mom will love that." I understood that my parents' willingness to come to me in Greece to be an affirmation of the new life I had chosen. I hoped that their visit would bring healing in our lives.

During that time, I was vaguely aware of an issue I kept pushing aside. I had no idea what I would do once the apartment was finished. I had come to Greece to write more boldly and to love more fully, yet I could do neither. I was afraid to even let myself think about falling in love again, because I feared that I might not survive another disappointment. And I could not write. At first I thought my writing block would pass, convincing myself that words must be forming inside me as I tackled yet another project in my home. But the words did not come. I felt that everything I had written was worthless, because, though my words had helped other women, they had not helped me.

I received several letters from a woman who was reading my books. She wrote that after overcoming her own despair, she had become a travel agent and longed to organize Goddess tours in Greece. I put her letters aside, thinking someday, maybe, I might lead a Goddess tour, but not now. I remembered teaching as exhausting. I had forgotten the ecstasy.

It began to dawn on me that my anger at the Goddess, my anger at life, my anger at love, my anger at myself, had become a bitterness that was clogging the well of my creativity. But knowing this did not help. As I went about my days, I had no desire to write. From time to time, I felt vaguely guilty, wondering if I ought to be trying harder, asking myself if I was denying a gift that had been given

uniquely to me. But when I thought about the two manu-
scripts I had written since moving to Greece, I felt nausea.
One of my editors wrote that my memoir of my first year in
Greece "passed the subway test"—she missed her stop while
reading it—but that, in the end, she felt she knew more than
the writer herself knew. I did not have the slightest clue what
was missing from the draft of the Goddess thealogy my editors had returned for revision. Nor did I want to think about
the Goddess who had betrayed my trust.

So I painted the pots on my balcony blue one day and
watched television in Greek the next, waiting for something
to happen, avoiding the question of what I was going to do
with the rest of my life.

Death

On the summer day I expected my mother to telephone saying that she and my dad had confirmed their reservations for Greece, she called instead to tell me that the persistent cough she had been complaining about had been diagnosed as cancer. She was going to start treatment, so she and my father would have to postpone their trip. In the next weeks, the prognosis worsened. There was cancer in her lungs, in her uterus, and in her hip bone. My brother Brian called to urge me to come home for Mom's seventy-second birthday in August. He said that though Mom remained optimistic, a doctor friend of the family told him, "This will be her last birthday, and she won't be here for Christmas." As I hastily packed, I took pictures of every nook and cranny of my new house to show to my mother.

When I saw Mom, it was hard to believe that she was dying. Although she had started chemotherapy and radiation, she looked beautiful and healthy. The illness had caused her to lose the extra pounds that had plagued her later years. Her hair had lightened to warm champagne beige. She was cheerful and full of life. She did not look or seem old. In her pink flowered dress with a low waistline and full skirt, she looked almost like a girl. Sadness in her eyes, evident in photographs taken at the time, was the only indication that she was not well.

When my mother was diagnosed in July with the cancer that took her life in December, she was as happy as she had ever been. My parents' economic struggles during the years of my brothers' and my childhoods were over. She had a beautiful home that she loved, and a garden filled with flowers that gave her endless joy. After my younger brother Kirk married and left home, my parents fell back in love. Recent years brought the birth of three new grandchildren. My father's retirement left my parents free to travel and enjoy life.

When I showed pictures of my new apartment to Mom, she seemed distracted. I guessed that her energies were engaged in the struggle with her illness, and I understood that she would never share my enthusiasm about my new home. I began to accept the fact that my parents' plan to come to Greece would have to substitute for their actually coming. Then my brother Brian picked up the photos and commented, "But this looks just like Mom's house." I was pleased to admit that he was right. Though Mom would never visit me in Greece, I would feel her presence in my home.

During my visit, Mom told us she didn't want to die and would fight for her life. She added that she had lived a very happy and blessed life and "if her time was up," she had "no regrets." I was relieved when she said she did not intend to be attached to tubes and had signed a living will stating that she did not want to be put into the hospital no matter how sick she might become. Mom confided to Brian that if it became clear that she would not recover, she didn't plan to linger. That was as close as she would come to talking about her death. Mom sent me back to Greece after three weeks, insisting that she felt fine and didn't need any help.

My mother's illness affected me more deeply than I had ever imagined it would. It is one thing to hear from a friend or to read that "the loss of a mother is the hardest loss you will ever face," that "your mother's death is something you will never get over," or that "the mother-child bond is the strongest bond." It is quite another to learn that what had sounded like clichés when spoken by others are deeply personal truths. Though I loved my mother and enjoyed being with her, it is also true that I left her when I went to college and never returned to live near her. For twenty-some years I had made my life apart from her: separated sometimes by the American continent; sometimes by the Atlantic Ocean;

but never by less than four hundred miles. I was quite unprepared for the depth of feeling her dying would evoke in me.

The knowledge that my mother was dying and that she might never ask for my help tormented me throughout the fall as I tried to go about my daily life in Athens. Whenever I spoke with my mother on the telephone, she insisted that she was "doing fine" and "didn't need help." In the late fall, my friend Susie made me realize that I was not calling my mother as frequently as I would have liked to because I was afraid that I would hear that she was getting worse. I sat down and wrote my mom the truth I had come to recognize: *I had never loved anyone as much as I loved her and nothing was more important to me than being with her in the time of her illness.*

Rereading the letter before sending it, I discovered as I would several times in the next months, that where I had meant to write that "nothing is more important than what is happening to *you* right now," I had instead written "than what is happening to *me.*" Shortly after mother died, I wrote a friend that "*I* died." Though I corrected my "mistakes," I realized that in another sense they were not "mistakes." Mom's dying was a passage I was experiencing with her. Though we were not, in any literal sense, the same person, it was also true that like the Mother and Daughter Goddesses, we were "in fact, merely the older and younger form of the same person; hence [the] easy confusion."[10]

18

My mother, who received cards and letters from her friends every day of her illness, said my letter "was the nicest letter" she had "ever received." It enabled her to call and tell me that she was not "doing fine" anymore, and she would like me to come "home."

When I arrived the Sunday before Thanksgiving, I was shocked to see that Mom had lost more weight, had very little appetite, took many seconds to get up from a chair, and was losing her hair from chemotherapy. Still, I was relieved to see that she got out of bed every morning, dressed herself, came down the stairs, and went out of the house almost every day. She insisted that a friend who was also suffering from cancer had looked much worse than she did, but was in remission. Her spirit was so strong; it was difficult not to believe her.

A few days later I heard my mother, standing at the kitchen sink in her light cotton robe, mutter to herself, "I hope I don't have to go through too much more of this." I took the opportunity to say, "Mom, if it gets too hard, I want you to know I am here to help you let go." Her response was abrupt, and her tone was harsh. "I don't want to talk about that," she said. "O.K.," I replied meekly and left the room. A few minutes later she came to me and apologized. "I don't want to talk about it," she repeated, "but I heard what you said, and I appreciate it." The only other acknowledgment Mom made of her dying in her last days was when she told me that she and her sister had "discussed it and decided that since neither of us had gone to church in thirty years, we don't expect that God will take much interest in us."

The doctor gave my mother a blood transfusion the day before Thanksgiving. I cooked the turkey for the first time, and Mom made it through the day with flying colors, putting on a silk dress and seeming almost well. On Sunday morning she said she wanted to go Christmas shopping with me. On Monday she and Dad and I went to lunch with one of her grandsons and took him to the airport. When we got home, she said she was tired and went upstairs to bed. She never really felt like getting up again. She slept a lot and ate very little.

By Tuesday night my mother needed oxygen. The tube did not hurt. Mom was still able to get up to go to the bathroom and even to come downstairs to watch television. Dad took her to the hospital on Thursday "to see if they could do anything." Apparently respecting my mother's wishes, the doctor did not admit her. After Mom died, Dad told me that this day was the first time the doctor had told him (and possibly the first time the doctor told my mother) that there was no longer any hope. I called my brothers, and they came over for dinner. Mom sat with us in the family room.

On Friday afternoon, Mom's friend Fran took me out to lunch alone after Mom said she didn't feel up to coming with us. A few months earlier, I had been invited to join

Fran, a round, motherly woman with silver grey hair, my mom, and their eighty-year-old friend Ruth, for a celebration of their August birthdays. We had gone to a fancy French restaurant and ordered whatever we wanted, including two glasses of wine each. When she dropped us back at the house, Fran had tried to give my mother a card "good for one hug." My mother had politely refused. As she hugged me that day, Fran whispered, "You are going to have some hard times. If you ever need anything, you can call on me."

Even though I scarcely knew Fran, I called and asked her to take me to lunch. I needed to cry and talk about my mother's dying. I hadn't been able to talk to anyone about it, because my mother had not been able to acknowledge that she was dying, and neither had my father. Fran and I held back nothing as we talked, ate, and drank several glasses of red wine. Fran spoke to me about her husband's dying. "I said goodbye to him after his stroke," she said, "because after that he never was himself again. Still, years later, when he slipped into a coma, he didn't seem to be able to let go. Finally the priest told me I had to go in and tell my husband that it was all right with me for him to die. He passed on soon afterwards."

On my way back from lunch, Fran told me that though we had only gotten to know each other since my mom's illness, she really liked me and felt we had an openness and ease in communication. She announced that she was going to "adopt" me. Later I understood my "adoption" to be a symbol and sign of the mystery I would learn as my mother was dying.

When we got back to the house, Mom sat up in bed and talked with the two of us for some time, even raising her nightgown and joking about her skinny legs. Fran told Mom she was wrong to think that God did not care about her. "God comes to anyone who asks Him," she insisted.

On Friday evening my brother Brian and I moved Mom's bed downstairs because the stairs made her short of breath. That night I worried that we might not hear her if she called, and I slept fitfully. Sometime during the night, I felt I saw my mother's mother, her father, her baby sister, and her own baby who had died waiting for her. Shortly before dawn, I heard Mom call. She was struggling for breath and asked me to turn up the oxygen. Dad came downstairs and turned it up, but it didn't help. As I understood that she was dying, I told Mom that "Grandma and Grandpa and baby Alice and baby Alan are waiting for you." Though she could not speak, she showed me with gestures that she heard me. *As my mother was dying, I had the absolutely clear sense that she was "going to love."* Not necessarily to Goddess or to God, not necessarily to her mother and father, but simply "to love." I told Mom several times not to be afraid because she was "going to love."

Remembering Fran's story, I turned to my father and said, "Dad, Fran says you must tell Mom that it's all right with you for her to die." He spoke quietly to her, and a few minutes later, she died, peacefully, in her own bed as she had chosen, with my dad and me sitting beside her, holding her hands.

The mystery I learned through my mother's dying cannot be reduced to a few simple words. Attempting to understand what had been revealed to me, I turned to a Hellenistic poem that found its way into the Bible.

If I speak in the tongues of humans or of angels
but have not love,
I am a noisy gong or clanging cymbal.
And if I have prophetic powers
and understand all mysteries and all knowledge,
and if I have all faith so as to move mountains,
but have not love,
I am nothing.
And if I give away all that I have,
and deliver my body to be burned,
but have not love,
I gain nothing.
Love is patient and kind,
love is not jealous or boastful,
it is not arrogant or rude.
Love does not insist on its own way;
it is not irritable or resentful;

it does not rejoice at wrong.
but rejoices in the right.
Love bears all things,
believes all things,
endures all things.
Love never ends . . .
So faith, hope, and love abide,
these three,
but the greatest of these is love. [11]

When my mother passed from this life she was surrounded by a great matrix of love. As she died, I began to understand that I too am surrounded by love and always have been. This is the great mystery.

Grief

*A*fter my mother's death, I spent several weeks with my father. A few days before she died, my mother said that she was pleased to hear my father and me laughing and talking downstairs. "I don't want to know what you were saying," she said, "I am just glad that you are getting along." I knew this was her way of telling me that she wanted us to comfort each other after she was gone. It was very hard to be together without Mom. And yet, our shared loss drew my dad and me closer than we had ever been. For the first time in my life, I saw my father cry. I could not help remembering that my mother had explained his outbursts of temper one summer in my early teens by telling me that dad had not been able to cry when his mother died. I will always treasure those days we spent together.

My friends Naomi and Ellen called almost every day to see how I was doing. That was a special gift. My adopted mother Fran was there to help me sort out my feelings of love and abandonment, to remind me that my mom loved me very much, and to give me her unqualified love.

A few weeks after Mom died, my friend and colleague of many years, Christine Downing, drove up to my parents' house to visit me. Over lunch in the grill room of my dad's club, I told Chris the story of Mom's dying. She was visibly moved. "I am working on a book on Demeter and Persephone," she said. "Not now, but in several months, I am going to send you a letter. In it, I will ask you to write the story of your mother's dying in relation to the myth of the Mother and Daughter Goddesses. You will sit down and write the essay in a couple of days." Chris was so calm and definite that I had the sense that her words came from a source outside herself. I remembered our conversation in the next days and months, and it comforted me to think of my story in relation to the stories of the Goddesses.

Just about the time that the Greeks have a memorial service marking the end of the first forty days of mourning, my father said I could go home. Back in Athens, I felt set apart. I spent a lot of time alone, watching television and working on my apartment. I cried a few tears every day when I thought of Mom—not the hysterical tears of abandonment so familiar to me, but simple tears of sadness and loss. I was aware that though my friends wanted to be helpful, they could not fully understand what I was going through. They had not yet lost their mothers, and they said truthfully that they were not ready even to think about what that loss would mean. During this time, I asked a friend's mother, whose own mother had died forty years earlier, if she still missed her mother. "Every day," was her simple answer.

My next-door neighbor, who lost her mother at about the same time, following Greek custom, would wear black for a year. I would have liked to wear black too, as an outward sign that I was going through a difficult time. In fact, I wore black more frequently than any other color that year.

In July, almost exactly a year after I learned that my mom had cancer, Chris's letter came. In it she asked me to expand what I had written about Demeter and Persephone in *Laughter of Aphrodite*. I imagined that she had forgotten what she said when we last met. I had not. I sat down and in a few days wrote the story of my mother's dying in relation to the myth of Demeter and Persephone.[12] As I wrote, the year of grieving, which had begun when I learned that my mother was dying, came to an end. I had also broken through my writing block.

On the evening of August fourteenth, I went with a friend to a little convent in the mountains of Evvoia to celebrate the "falling asleep" of the Panagia, the death and assumption of the Mother of God. The nuns had decorated an icon that showed the Panagia lying in her deathbed with flowers. As I gazed at the icon, the Panagia's image merged with my mother. I kissed the Panagia, cried, and said good-bye to Mom.

Not long after, I was asked to speak to a group of women and men who were on a Myth and Mystery tour of the Mediterranean. I would meet them at Eleusis, site of the Eleusinian mysteries, dedicated to the Mother and Daughter, Demeter and Persephone. I wasn't sure what would be asked of me there, or what I would say. As I left home, I tucked the story of my mother's dying into my blue bag with the thought that I might read it there. As it turned out, the tour leaders had been told that only a licensed Greek guide could speak about the archaeology of the site, and they did not think a ritual would be appropriate. So the only thing left was for me to read my story.

I led the group to a sheltered place where there is a crevice in the rock. On this spot, it is said, the Earth opened up while Persephone was picking flowers, allowing Hades to abduct her to the underworld. Several years earlier, my friend Judy left her mother's ashes in the opening, returning her mother to the womb of the Mother. I thought of Judy as I sat on a stone near the crevice. Someone set a bouquet of lavender mums on a rock next to me. The others gathered close around me as I told the story of my mother's dying. My voice cracked several times, and I had to pause, fighting back tears. When I finished, I could feel that everyone was with me. Some of them, both women and men, were reliving their mothers' deaths. Others were anticipating the great loss. Few eyes were dry. My story had become part of a ritual, shared with others. I was no longer alone. It was appropriate that my healing continued at Eleusis, where stories of mothers and daughters, loss and reunion, death and rebirth, had been told. I offered a lavender mum to each of the others, saying, "Leave your flower here on these ancient stones, or take it home as a memory of this sacred moment."

Part Two

PREPARATION

If you are squeamish

*Don't prod the
beach rubble.*[13]

The Sacred Myrtle Tree

*T*hough my mother's death catalyzed a deep internal shift, it would take time for it to unfold. I still was angry and hurt. I had broken through my writing block, but I was not ready to begin another project. I had told my story in a sacred place, but I did not yet trust the Goddess. Still deeply depressed, I did not feel moved to join my friends at a conference in Crete on The Future of Partnership, organized with the intention of bringing "the partnership vision" of the peaceful, Goddess-oriented, egalitarian culture of ancient Crete into the modern world. My colleagues and Goddess friends, Mara and Naomi, as well as my editor, Marie, were travelling half way around the world to come to the conference; they hinted that they would not forgive me if I did not come to a conference that was occurring in my own back yard. Once again, I was dragged "kicking and screaming" to a place where I would find healing. The travel agent who wanted me to lead Goddess pilgrimages would also attend the conference, but I had warned her that it was unlikely that I would agree to lead a tour any time soon.

The magic began when, on the conference's free day, five of us set out in a rented car to explore the island. We had only been on the road for about forty minutes when we saw a sign pointing left that said "Paliani Nunnery." Four of the five of us agreed to make the detour, so we set off down a winding dirt road that climbed up the side of a hill.

The Paliani nunnery is built around an open court with a church in its center. The steps leading to the cells that ring the courtyard were filled with pots of flowers in bloom: sweet-smelling basil, gaudy pink geraniums, and intoxicatingly aromatic white jasmine. The black-clad nuns all seemed to be less than five feet tall and very old. Naomi at four-foot-ten must have felt she had come home. I felt like Alice-in-Wonderland.

The sound of running water drew us to the Panagia Myrtia, a very old myrtle tree with shoots sprouting from the roots curving upward to form a massive, intricately woven trunk. A stone wall encloses the sacred space around the tree, and a small icon of the Panagia, the All Holy, the Mother of God, in a glass case is attached to its trunk. Crutches and body braces hang from the branches of the tree, testimony to the healing power of the All Holy Myrtia. A hand-lettered sign written in Greek said: "Please pick only dry branches from the tree. Those who do so will be blessed." I deciphered this for the others, and enchanted, we each picked a small twig.

We were approached by a sweet-faced nun, shorter than Naomi, who told us she was the youngest of the nuns. "Almost all of the sisters are very old and most of them are sick," she said. "No one has joined us in many years. "But what will happen to the tree and this place if no one else joins?" I asked. "The Panagia will provide a solution," she replied determinedly. "We pray for it every day," she added. "This tree is holy," she continued, "because the icon of the Panagia was found in it. When they tried to put it in the church, it kept returning at night to the tree. Finally the people understood that the icon wanted to be worshipped in her tree. This tree is over one thousand years old. Put a twig from the tree in your car when you leave," she cautioned us. "It will protect you on the road."

The nun unlocked the door of the church with a large iron key and pointed us to the icon of the Panagia on the iconostasis in front of the church, on the left side. It is a life-sized painting on wood of the Mother and Child. Her robe is deep dark red, and across it are stretched two long chains on which earrings, rings, bracelets, and other votive offerings are suspended. One gift of two ornate silver haloes crowns the heads of the mother and baby. There are also four silver hands and two tiny silver feet affixed to the icon.[14] I held up my hand and discovered it was exactly the same size as the silver hand of the Panagia that rests against her robe just under her breast, where it points, perhaps, to her baby.

We approached the icon in turn. Each of us felt her power—even Mardy, who had not wanted to come to the convent, and Naomi, who calls herself a Jewish atheist. "That icon seems very alive," I said to the nun who waited near the door of the church. "I felt an energy field all around it." "It is powerful," she confirmed. "It has performed many miracles. You can see all of the jewelry that has been offered to her." "I've often wondered about that," I said. "Are the gifts given when you make the prayer or after it has been answered?" "After," she said determinedly. "The purpose of the gift is to declare the icon's power. Just recently a couple came here to baptize their baby. They brought a big candle. This couple, who live in Athens, are both doctors. They had been married for seventeen years without having a baby. They had tried everything. Finally, they came here and prayed. A year to the day later, the woman gave birth to a son. That is why they brought the baby here to be baptized. Yes, this icon has performed many miracles." I translated for my friends, each of whom, in her own way, allowed herself to believe that maybe, just maybe, the icon would work her miracles for us.

We each bought a candle, approached the icon, and made a secret prayer. As I stood before the Panagia with the silver hands, I was moved to ask for something I had given up hope of ever finding. When Naomi turned back toward me, I could see that her eyes were wet. "What did you pray for?" I asked. "I can't tell," was all she would say. In the end none of us spoke of what we had asked for. That seemed to be part of the mystery. Leaving the monastery, we remarked on how lucky it had been that we saw the sign and turned left off the main road.

Mysteries

*A*fter the conference we set out to visit the caves of Eilitheia in Amnissos and Agia Paraskevi in Skoteino. As we drove along the coast toward Amnissos, I recalled that caves have been understood as sacred from the dawn of religion. When people knew the earth as their mother, the cave, the opening in the earth, was her vagina and womb, the passageway to her deepest mysteries, the secrets of birth and rebirth.

The Eilitheia Cave is in the hills above the ancient port of Amnissos. We arrived in the morning, accompanied by the guard who came with us to unlock the gate. The cave has one large, long room, with a wide mouth, and a low ceiling. There is a belly stone near the entrance that women rubbed to insure conception. At the center of the cave, in shadowy darkness, are two stalagmites, one squat and the other tall, surrounded by the remains of ancient walls that enclosed

the sacred space. The guard told us that they were worshipped as the Mother, seated, and the Daughter, standing.
Their heads were chopped off with the blow of an ax.[15] In
the back of the cave there are small pools of water, used for
healing

As our eyes adjusted to the darkness, we felt that we too
had entered into the womb of the Mother. Naomi sat by the
Daughter stalagmite, while I leaned against the Mother. We
chanted to Her and sang, aware of the bemused but accepting presence of the guard, who retreated to the entrance of
the cave. As we turned to leave, Mara crouched at the cave's
entrance to take a picture, her short, full body the image of
the Mother Goddess, her wispy blonde hair capturing the
light, crowning her like a halo. Slowly, we emerged from the
cool depths, the place of ancient mysteries, into the light and
warmth of the midday sun.

We visited the Skoteino Cave late in the day, after lunch
and a refreshing swim in the sea. To reach the cave, we as-
cended into the mountains, passed through the small village
of Skoteino, and turned right down a dirt road. Above the
cave is a small church dedicated to Agia Paraskevi, the patron saint of eyesight. I had been to the cave eleven years earlier with my husband, Roger, on the saint's name day, July
26th. That day the locals celebrated first in the church, where
they decorated the icon of Agia Paraskevi with flowers and lit
candles, and then in the cave, where they roasted lamb, sang,

and danced. It is likely that this cave has a continuity of worship from ancient times to the present day.

The first time I visited the cave of Skoteino, which means dark, I thought it was a single, huge, high-ceilinged, cathedral-like room, adorned with stalagmites and stalactites. In the meantime, I had learned that beyond the first room, there are three more levels, the final one, totally dark. Mardy offered to lead the way. Two young German men, emerging from the depths, told us the way down was not easy, as there was no clear path.

Marie, unsure of her footing, stayed near the entrance. Naomi, afraid of the unknown, perched on a rock at the back of the first room holding her candle. Mara, Mardy, and I braved the descent. We did not know what awaited us in the dark. With candles and small flashlights, we climbed and slid, sensing a way down. The rocks were cool, damp in some places, but not slippery. There were no sharp edges because the rocks had been smoothed by water. Encouraging each other, we reached a place where it looked like the next descent would be though a hole. We still had faint light from the mouth of the cave. The final passageway was unknown, frightening, inviting. We paused, eyes fixed on the dark opening. Mardy broke the silence saying that we should turn back because the sun was about to set.

I made the ascent more rapidly than the others, my body urging me on until I reached the first level. As I walked slowly up the path that meandered through the first large room, I could see two women before me with candles, and two behind me coming up from the depths. I could almost see Persephone coming up from the underworld, torch in hand. Surely it was in a place like this that the Eleusinian Mysteries began.[16]

Dionysian Rites

*T*hat evening, Naomi and I dropped the others back in Heraklion to catch their planes, while we set off to spend three more nights and days in Crete. We hoped to spend the first night in the guest rooms at Paliani, but when we arrived, the convent was closed, the gates locked tight. We could not arouse a single nun, though we knocked loudly and called out. In the nearby town we asked someone to call the nunnery, but there was no answer. There were no hotels or rooms to rent in the nearby towns, so we drove on through the night to the next day's destination, Zaros, which had been recommended to us by a waiter who served us in Heraklion.

Zaros is in the Psiloritis mountains, also known as the Idean range, not far from Phaistos, and closer still to the Kamares Cave, where pilgrims left offerings of beautiful black, red, and white pottery known as Kamares ware. Our hotel had a working water mill, patronized by old farmers with donkeys.[17] Its taverna serves freshwater trout and salmon trout raised in ponds fed by the mountain spring.

We planned to climb to the Kamares Cave the next day, but when we discovered that it was a four-hour uphill walk on an unmarked trail with very little tree cover, we decided instead to hike the Zaros Gorge, which because of its water source was shaded by many trees. The Psiloritis Mountains are bare rock, whitish and grey above the tree line, wild, yet worn by time. We found we could simply sit and gaze at them, and so we spent our first day in the hotel's garden by the pool.

We had a scrumptious dinner of fresh fish, salad, fried potatoes, local amber-colored wine, and tiny olives. Instead of fresh bread, we were offered paximadia (rusks) and shown how to float them in bowls of water until just soft enough to eat. One of the waiters brought us a pitcher of wine offered by a local shepherd we had seen earlier with two new-born lambs. Soon the two waiters, Themis and Nikos, bearing more wine, sat down at our table. They told us they were best friends and had just gotten out of the army. When they discovered that we were writers, the two young men were intrigued. "Our village has a very interesting history and many interesting customs," they told us. "If you would like to come back and write about it, we will introduce you to all of the old people." This conversation was in Greek, but I translated for Naomi. "This must indeed be a very interesting village," I said to her, "because when they learn that I am a writer, most Greek men say 'write about me, I have a very interesting story.' These men, in contrast, want us to write about their village."

When we finished the wine, the young men offered to give us a lift back to our hotel on their motorbikes, suggesting we could have a coffee at the hotel bar. When we got to the hotel, they didn't stop. "What happened?" I asked. "The bar wasn't open at the hotel, so we're looking for another place." I wondered what Naomi, perched on the back of a motorbike and unable to speak Greek, must be thinking—especially since she was afraid of the unknown. We drove through the town and turned down a dirt road, arriving at the Zaros water factory. "We wanted to show you this," they said sheepishly. "People drink our water all over Crete." "O.K.," Naomi said, "but then you must take us back." There were a few workers on the night shift, and the boys told us they had worked there too, before going into the army.

Leaving the factory, we continued down the dirt road heading away from the town. "Where are we going?" I asked, wondering what we had gotten ourselves into. "Just a minute," Themis said, as he got off the bike in front of what looked like a small house in the middle of nowhere. "We need to go back," Naomi said definitively. "Yes, I already said that," I answered. "Come inside," Themis beckoned. "We want to show you how they make the raki," the colorless alcoholic drink that had been offered to us in shot glasses after meals. "This is the still," he continued, as he showed us into a small dark room with a glowing fire. "After the wine is pressed, they put the skins and stems into barrels like those you see in the corner. The mixture takes six weeks to ferment, and then they bring it to a still, where it is heated over a fire. The steam that rises is directed through long curved pipes, and comes out as raki," he said, pointing to various parts of the mechanism.

"I want to go home now," Naomi said. "First you must take the raki," the boys insisted, guiding us through a narrow doorway into a second, somewhat larger room. A couple of men rose and offered us their Greek-style chairs. Raki was passed to us, followed by potatoes baked in the fire, seasoned with lemon and salt, to be eaten with the fingers, and passed on. "They say they are sorry, but they have eaten all the meat," Nikos said apologetically. Naomi was about to insist again that she wanted to leave, but at that very moment, she was passed half of a juicy red pomegranate. She took a few seeds and ate them, passing the pomegranate on to me. "I guess this means we stay," she said, "like Persephone."

"Kostas is the best singer in Zaros," Nikos said, pointing to a small wiry man with a moustache, who was singing plaintively while playing the Cretan lyra, a kind of violin played like a fiddle. The young boy with curly dark hair and round eyes played an instrument that looked like a guitar. "He is just learning," one of the boys said. "Zaros has the best singers in the whole area. They play in all the villages."

We were told that the Cretan songs called *mantinadas* are based on rhyming couplets, which may be sung by one man, followed by another, and so on around the room, as the singers weigh up who is singing about the prettiest girl, and who has suffered the most for his love. The boys explained that whoever is distilling raki must throw a party for his friends and welcome anyone who turns up. Our party included many of the young men of the village, but on another night, in another still, the party might be for the older men. Women were not usually invited. Naomi and I were impressed by the warmth and affection the men expressed for each other. Many of them sat unselfconsciously with their arms around each other, as our young men did from time to time, too. We felt privileged to be included in a men's mystery. "Robert Bly, eat your heart out," Naomi whispered to me. "This is the real thing."

Nikos and Themis offered translations of the songs from the Cretan dialect into Greek, eager that we understand everything. While Naomi and I had expected songs of wild men out of the mountains, violence, and vendettas, we were pleasantly surprised to learn that most of the songs were about unrequited love. "I have worn out many pairs of shoes climbing the mountains to get a glimpse of her," sang one. "My goats' udders are sore because I sit and think of my girl when I should be milking my flock," replied another. Cups of raki, potatoes, and pomegranates continued to be passed around.

"We don't sing like this in America," Naomi commented. "That's too bad," Nikos responded. "We sing out our joy and our pain. What do you do with yours?" What indeed, we wondered, as we sat in a dark room, entranced by unfamiliar rhythms, unexpected feelings. "This is not the underworld," one of us said to the other, as we were pulled up to dance. "This is the Dionysian festival." We were being shown a mystery.

Challenge

I had agreed to meet Carol, the travel agent who loved my
work, in Athens on my return, and when I did, I found
that I had changed my mind about leading a Goddess Pilgrimage. "I will do it," I said, "but only if it is in Crete." This
was not what Carol had in mind—she had visualized the
Parthenon, Eleusis, and Delphi. But as she had no choice,
she agreed to organize a Goddess Pilgrimage in Crete.[18]

I secured a library pass from the American Classical
School in Athens, and spent much of the winter reading
about the history and archaeology of Crete. In the spring,
I would travel to Crete to map out the itinerary for the
tour. I hoped that one of my friends would come with me,
but in the end I realized I would have to go by myself.
Though I lived alone, I had a number of fears about travelling alone. I knew I would be doing a lot of driving, and
I hoped I would not get tired. I felt embarrassed to eat

alone in restaurants, and wondered what others would think of me. I wanted to go back to the Skoteino Cave, but I was thought it might be dangerous as I would not have anyone with me. As I later realized, all of these small fears were standing in for the big fear that I would have to spend the rest of my life alone.

The day before I was to leave for Crete, I found myself slipping into despair. I was trying so hard to accept my life as it was, trying not to long for the companion I did not have, and felt I would never have. Going to Crete alone made me feel vulnerable. Without warning, I began to hear the voice that I had worked so hard to suppress, telling me that *"No one understands you, no one will ever love you, you will always be alone. It is just too difficult. You might as well die."*

When my Greek friend Melpo and I met for dinner that night, she sensed my depression. "The way you feel is not right," she said to me as I picked at the black-eyed peas we had ordered at a local tavern. "If I were going to Crete tomorrow, I would be happy. But I have to stay in Athens and work in a bank. I'd love to be as free as you are. I am going to tell you something you may not want to hear. Sometimes I feel the way you do, but I have decided to help myself. I think you should join my therapy group. I think you need to help yourself too." I recalled our recent conversations about the therapy group. I always found something that helped me in the stories Melpo told. Still, I was skeptical. "I have tried therapy," I began, "and it didn't help.

"I know what my problems are, but it doesn't do me any good to know. I feel that life has passed me by. It's too late. I will always be alone," I concluded, even as I realized that I sounded tense, bitter, and close to tears. "Don't you think I have been in therapy many times too," Melpo rejoined. "Don't you think I know many therapists are stupid? But in this group I am changing. You know that. Last year I didn't even want to be around women. The group helped me to see that my father taught me to hate women. I am a woman too. He taught me to hate myself. I think this group can help you."

I looked at the tall, determined, sometimes intimidating woman sitting across from me. I thought back to the many times she had cancelled plans we made. I knew she probably would not be having dinner with me if she hadn't started to like women. I tried another tack. "I don't think my Greek is good enough for a Greek therapy group." Melpo's response was blunt: "If you want to help yourself, your Greek is fine. If you don't, it will never be good enough."

Trusting the Dark

*T*o my surprise, once in Crete, I enjoyed getting into the car each day and going exactly where I wanted to go at my own pace. I did get tired driving, so I rested for two days at the seaside village of Mochlos. Naomi, who would have loved to make the journey with me, asked me to write a journal of my travels for her, and between that and planning the next day's itinerary, I had plenty to do at meals. I felt that Naomi was travelling with me, as I wrote her of my adventures.

A few days into my trip, I decided to return to Skoteino. On the way to the cave, I thought about those who had come there before me. For the early settlers of Crete in the Neolithic era, caves provided shelter from wind, rain, and summer heat. These first immigrants buried or stored the bones of their ancestors in caves. They must have prayed and conducted rituals in caves, as their ancestors had done before them, and their descendants would do after them. For many millennia, people made a connection between the womb of woman and the womb of earth: they understood that life emerges from darkness and hoped that what is dead—whether seeds, bones, or the human heart—can be reborn in the dark.

When I arrived at the Skoteino Cave, it was the middle of the afternoon. There was no one else in sight. I imagined that if I fell or broke a bone, it would be days before anyone might find me. I was afraid; yet I knew I had already made it to the third level. Praying for protection in the little church of Agia Paraskevi, I decided to go as far as I felt safe. I would descend with a candle and extra matches, leaving my flashlight behind. I quickly made my way to the end of the first level. From there I slowly climbed and slid over rocks in semi-darkness. My fear and anticipation melted into a solemn determination. No sisterly giggles this time.

After a while I found myself at the edge of the second level, looking down a steep rock face to the third level, a large round room with stalactite formations emerging from the shadows of the wall high above me, capturing the last light from the mouth of the cave. From where I sat, I could see the dark hole that appeared to be the opening to the fourth level. I felt it would be dangerous to go any farther, so I decided I would stay where I was, sitting on the rocks looking down. I was very pleased to have gotten this far on my own.

I asked the Goddess of Skoteino what I was meant to do with the rest of my life. My writing block was broken, but I had not started writing again. If I wasn't going to write, what was I going to do? I asked my question again and again. I felt the power of the cave and my own power in conquering my fear. But I didn't hear an answer to my prayer.

The third level beckoned to me. I decided to ask if it was safe to go any farther. I immediately received an answer: *"Stay close to the rocks, and you will find your way."* I understood this to mean that if I stayed close to the walls of the cave, where I could lean against the rocks for support if necessary, I would find a safe path. I made my way to the third level easily and went to the dark place, the opening to the fourth level. I started to slide down. The passage was the length and width of a double staircase, with a sheer drop at its beginning.

Soon, I was in total darkness. One more turn, and my candle lit up a large stalagmite formation: the imageless image of the Goddess. The formation stood in the center of a large round room, perhaps twenty feet wide, with very high ceilings. It formation was taller than I was and at least six feet in diameter. I sat on the floor of the cave, leaning against Her, and extinguished my candle. It was completely dark. I had reached the center. I was in the womb of the Goddess. I repeated my prayers. I don't know which was more powerful:

this place, or conquering my fears in order to get there. I supposed it had always been a combination of the two.

In the silence, I heard sounds at the entrance of the cave. I thought others had come, so I began my ascent. When I reached the mouth of the cave, I realized that sounds were the cooing of pigeons that lived in the crevices of the rocks. As I emerged from the depths, I knew this was a journey I had to make alone. I might not have received an answer to my questions, but I felt an inner strength I had not known before.

Flowers of Spring

*T*oward the end of my journey to find the path of the pilgrimage, I returned to Zaros, stopping at the Paliani nunnery on the way. I had learned that the nunnery was known as ancient (*palia*) in 668 C.E. when mention of it was first made in extant records. When I arrived, the convent was teeming with new life. Bees buzzed around the flowers that spilled out of pots on the steps leading up to the cells. The Sacred Myrtle Tree was sprouting with new growth and in bloom: it was covered with hundreds of tiny white blossoms with cascading stamens.

I looked for the sweet nun with whom we had spoken in the fall and learned that her name is Evgenia, the Gracious One. She greeted me warmly and introduced me to the abbess, who gave me a cross carved from myrtle wood: to me it looked like a woman with upraised arms. She also gave me a photograph of the icon of the Panagia. The nuns insisted I stay for lunch.

I imagined a communal meal at the long table in the refectory, so I was surprised to be served alone in the kitchen behind it. "All the nuns cook and eat in their own cells," I was told. I would discover that this was part of the "own rhythm" style of monastic organization that preceded more rigid systems. My lunch was fresh artichoke hearts and potatoes stewed in tomatoes and olive oil, thick slices of bread, and feta cheese. I learned that the nuns had once farmed their own plots of land, but now that they are all old, the convent rents the land to others in exchange for fruits and vegetables, olives, oil, and cheese. After my lunch, I reluctantly left the convent.

If I had wondered whether the mountains of Zaros would still move me, I found my answer that day on a late afternoon walk down a farm road. The power of the mountains towering above me was palpable. The next day I hiked the gorge again. It was even more beautiful in the spring. Chamomile, thyme, sage, oregano, and other fragrant herbs and flowers grew along the trail, filling the air with a scent that reminded me ever so faintly of maple syrup. Alone on the trail, I began to sing. "The hills are alive with the sound of music." "We all come from the Goddess." And, "She changes everything she touches, and everything She touches changes." Gurgling water appeared in the riverbed about half way up the trail. I stopped frequently to gaze at the white and grey rock formations that enclosed the gorge. I felt called to give thanks for being alone in the mountain on this day.

On my way back from Zaros, I stopped again at the nunnery. This time, I was greeted as an old friend by gentle, intelligent Evgenia and her robust cellmate Kaliniki, Good Victory. I sat with them in the small kitchen of their three-room cell, which included a reception room and kitchen on the main level, and upstairs a small bedroom with three narrow beds. Kaliniki was cleaning artichokes. Evgenia offered me chocolates and sweet bread. We laughed that all of the doorways were far less than my height. "I could never live here," we joked. While I knew that in other ways too I could never live here, part of me wanted to. I wondered if the Panagia, the All Holy Mother of All, would call me to help the nuns or in some other way make me part of her plan for the survival of the Sacred Myrtle Tree.

Gifts

When I returned to Athens a few days later, I unpacked a copy of the larger of the two Snake Goddesses found at Knossos. She wears a long skirt and an embroidered apron; a tight bodice accentuates her full bare breasts. A large snake crawls up one of her outstretched arms, down her back, over her shoulders, and down her other arm. A second snake slithers around her breasts, encircles her belly, and comes to rest on her tall headdress. Her eyes stare calmly ahead. I set her on the buffet in my dining room, next to her sister. She too wears a tight bodice, full skirt, and embroidered apron. She appears to be in trance, and she holds two small writhing snakes in her upraised hands.

The Snake Goddesses from Crete call to mind a time when women were not afraid, when our power to bring life forth from the darkness was recognized as sacred. I stepped back to get a better view of the two Goddesses guarding the center of my home. Gazing at them, I seemed to hear a sigh of relief: as if they were saying, *"We belong together. We do not like to be apart."*

I continued to unpack, placing a blue bowl sculpted with birds in the center of the table, in front of the Goddesses. I arranged twigs from the Sacred Myrtle Tree at Paliani, stones and pottery shards, and dried herbs and flowers from the mountains, in the bowl, and set it on a circle of lace crocheted by one of the nuns. A silver-framed photograph of my mother laughing, and a second, of her mother, were already there, along with three pairs of my mother's ceramic birds. I bought a silver frame for the photograph of the Paliani Panagia, and set her on the other side of the buffet. I remembered that the Snake Goddesses were found with shells, suggesting their connection to the sea. I found my collection of shells in a box and set four striated ones around the bowl. The composition lacked balance. Reluctantly, I selected two rose-colored shells from my Aphrodite rituals in Lesbos. It took me a couple of days to realize that I had unconsciously created an altar. I added three pink candles and two dark blue votive lights, dedicating the altar to the Cretan Goddess in her many forms. Lighting the candles, I opened myself to Her.

A few days later, in a letter to a friend, I wrote, "I see myself spending more and more time in Crete, exploring the sacred mountains and sacred caves, returning to visit the sacred tree, learning about archaeology and folklore, possibly one day buying a house in Crete and spending part of each year there." As I reread the words I had written, I understood that when the Goddess of the Skoteino Cave said: *"Stay close to the rocks, and you will find your way,"* She had answered my question. The words also meant: *"Stay close to the mountains and caves of Crete, and you will find the path of your life."*

Promise

As I settled back into my life in Athens, I felt transformed in ways I could not fully name. Traveling alone in Crete and descending into the darkness of the cave had given me the courage to face whatever was dark and unknown inside me. I was ready to stalk my despair in therapy.

I met Charis Kataki, the leader of the therapy group my Greek friend Melpo recommended, for an initial private appointment. Her office was in a house on a residential street in an upper-middle class suburb of Athens. I was early for the appointment and waited nervously. When Charis opened the door of her sunny, plant-filled office, I took in her external appearance: attractive rather than beautiful, elegantly dressed, short, light-haired, several years older than myself. As we sat down, Charis told me that she had studied in America, and invited me to speak in English if I would feel more comfortable. I said I would rather speak Greek, so she could get a sense of how I might do in the group.

Since Melpo had told me that Charis was married and had children, I assumed she would find little to empathize with in my story, but I plunged ahead. I felt bitter about my life. I found it too difficult to live alone. If I had known that I might have to make a choice between love and work, I would have chosen love. I felt the feminist movement had betrayed me when it said that I could have it all. I had ended up with nothing. As a Goddess scholar, I could not find a satisfying academic job. My writing, once a lifeline, felt meaningless. It was too late to have children. Maybe I was already too old to meet anyone. I spoke of the voice inside me that says: *"No one understands me, no one will ever love me, I might as well die."* I said it felt like that voice came from a separate person over whom I had no control. I was afraid that one day I might commit suicide. Charis asked me about my parents, my education, my marriage, my decision to live in Greece.

"You made the right choice when you moved to Greece," she stated when I had finished speaking. "Greeks live from here," she said, touching her belly. "You needed to learn that." Then she looked me in the eyes and said simply: *"No one should have to live with the kind of despair you feel."* I was stunned. No one had ever told me that before. Charis said that she knew I had tried everything I could think of to change my life—from therapy to changing my country, to changing the world, and even changing God. She promised that the group would help me to face the source of my despair so that I could move beyond it. That didn't seem possible. I had always assumed that the sadness I felt was normal—or alternatively that it was too deeply rooted in me to change.

I was intrigued. Could I feel differently?

Insight

When I was asked to tell the group what had brought me to therapy, I began to speak about the feelings that had plagued me since my love affair with Andreas ended. Charis, whose style is abrupt—some would say unsympathetic—cut me off in mid-sentence. *"The feelings you had when Andreas left you were too extreme. They were not about him."* After a pregnant pause, she continued, *"Didn't you say your father was an alcoholic?*

I was stunned. "I said my grandfather drank too much," I stammered. "A friend once suggested that my father's personality was shaped by his father's alcoholism. Because his father was often out of control, my father must have felt he must always be in control." "Talk to us about your father," Charis interjected. "My father and I are very different," I began. "He is a traditional patriarchal father figure, I am a feminist. He is right-wing. I am left-wing. I think he loves me, but I don't know if he is proud of what I have accomplished." "I don't think you are so different," Charis interjected. "I know we are alike in many ways," I continued. "We are both very intelligent. We both work very hard. We are both demanding of ourselves and others."

I stopped and then began again. "I thought my father and I were becoming close after my mother's death. We talked openly for the first time in years, maybe for the first time ever. We shared our grief and our love for Mom. He told me he couldn't share his feelings with my brothers, but he could with me. I thought we had made a break-through. Just before I left, he gave me my mother's beautiful antique gold watch. But then, the other shoe dropped. My father began to tell me all of the ways I had irritated him over the weeks we had been together. I kept moving a chair in the kitchen, and one night he tripped over it. I was stunned. I thought I was putting the chair back where it belonged. Another example of my 'aggressive behavior' occurred while I was making dinner for friends of the family. I said, 'Dad will set the table,' instead of asking him nicely. I felt I had spoken in a friendly way. I broke into tears. I had been trying so hard to get along with my dad. I thought I had succeeded, but I had not. My dad got up and left the room. I cried all night long. I started to wonder if either he or my mother had ever loved me. Something about that night felt familiar. My father's behavior is unpredictable. Just when I feel we are getting along, something causes him to explode. When I am trying to do the right thing, he finds something to criticize. I can never please him."

I took a deep breath. Charis and her co-therapist, Patrick, a gentle Frenchman, who like me was a foreigner in Greece, asked me questions about my relationship with my father. Finally Patrick was satisfied. "I think I see the dynamics of your family myth," he announced. "Because his father was an alcoholic, your father felt that there was something 'bad' that could be passed down in the male side of his family line. For some reason we don't know, he thought that this 'badness' would harm the girls in the family. This was a family myth. It wasn't true," Patrick said, looking at me intently from behind his thick glasses.

"But your father believed it was. So whenever he felt close to you, he created a distance. Your perceptions were not wrong. It was precisely when your father felt love for you that he withdrew, got angry, or criticized." Patrick paused again "This must have been very confusing for you as a little child. The truth is that your father loves you very much. But he can't allow himself to feel close to you, for fear of harming you. If you can understand this, perhaps it won't hurt so much from now on," he concluded, smiling tentatively and nodding, as if to ask me if I understood.

Patrick offered this depiction of my father's family myth shortly after I began therapy. On one level, it sounded a bit too clear and too simple, but on another, it felt right. The more I thought it, the more it made sense. I began to fill in details Patrick did not know. I had not mentioned that my father's brother died of his alcoholism: my father probably felt this was "proof" that badness is passed to the males in the family. My father's sister had been harmed by her father. She had a nervous breakdown when I was a child and became addicted to tranquilizers. Her husband told me that my aunt's problems stemmed from father's refusal to let her go to college—that probably was not the first time her desires and hopes had been thwarted by her father. My father often expressed his fear that my brother Brian would "go bad" like his brother. He must have been unconsciously terrified that I would "fall apart" like his sister. His sacrifices to pay for my education may have been his way of making up for his father's mistakes. I began to see that my father was the only one of his siblings who had managed to "hold it together." The other two had gone "out of control." No wonder my father struggled so hard to stay in control of everything and everyone. He had done so at great cost to himself and others, but he had survived. Both of his siblings were dead.

The family myth explained why my younger brother Kirk had been drawn to Mormonism, a religion that prohibits alcohol and stresses self-control on the part of males. The patterns Patrick described illuminated my relationships with men. Many of the men I loved were deeply unhappy. I must have felt that if I could heal their pain, I could heal my father's too, and then I would receive his love. In addition, my father's pattern of withdrawing love precisely when he felt it the most, made it almost impossible for me to make a realistic assessment of relationships. Love and rejection were so deeply entwined in my experience that I could not tell the difference between them. Moreover, my mother constantly told me that my father loved me, but just didn't know how to show it. This was a prescription for accepting unloving behavior on the part of the men I loved.

Over the next months, this new knowledge began to take root in my body and in my feelings. I began to understand that though I was loved, I had not always been treated in a loving way. Before it had been one or the other—either I was loved and lovable; or I was unloved and unlovable. I began to see that I had been loved, but also deeply harmed by my father's erratic behavior.

Slowly, the feeling that I was unlovable began to dissolve. As this happened, the dynamics of all my other relationships began to change. When I stopped looking for verification that I was worthy of love, I began to see others more clearly. It was as if I had gone through life with a veil over my eyes, and the veil had been lifted. For the first time in my life, I was able to separate myself from others. I was able to see that, just as I, as a little child, had not caused my father's reactions to me, neither was I, for the most part, responsible for other people's behavior. I began to see that when others disappointed me, more often than not, it was because of their limitations or choices, not mine. This insight was incredibly freeing.

I would fall back into my old patterns, but those times would become fewer. The balance was shifting.

Words with You

*I*n the middle of summer, I was called back to Mithymna, to Lesbos, to the place where I had felt claimed as a priestess of Aphrodite, the place where I trusted and served Her, the place where I began the love affair, that when it ended, plunged me into despair that consumed my will to live and closed the wellsprings of my creativity.

I had been asked to give two lectures to a group of graduate students studying archetypal psychology and Greek mythology. I was uneasy about returning to Mithymna after an absence of four years. I felt abandoned by friends from the village who had not written or called. I was still very angry at Aphrodite, yet I had agreed to speak about Her to the group in Lesbos. I was angry with myself for letting myself become so disappointed in love. It would hurt to return to the place where I had lost so much.

Three nights before I was due to leave for Lesbos, while looking at a framed print of the Panagia Myrtia, the Panagia of the Myrtle Tree, I started to wonder if myrtle trees could really grow to be a thousand years old. I decided to look up myrtle trees in a book. To my great surprise and distress, I read that myrtle trees were sacred to Aphrodite.[19] Given how angry I was with Aphrodite, I felt this was a very dirty trick. "My" tree was "Hers." I didn't want Her to have anything to do with my new altar, my renewed relationship with the Goddess, or with my twigs from the sacred tree. I was furious. I began to feel heavy and depressed. I left my air-conditioned study and went to the altar in my living room. I lit candles, hoping this act would release my feelings. It was over 100 degrees outside and my living room was very hot, so I returned to my study. There, I flipped through another book, my attention coming to rest on a chapter about Hermes, the trickster. I began to feel agitated.

I returned to the living room, faced the altar and began having words with Aphrodite. "I hate you," I said. "*Se miso*," I repeated over and over again in Greek and English. "I hate you. *Se miso*. You abandoned me," I continued. "You left me to die. Not once, but many times. You left me in the underworld. All I did was love you, worship you and introduce others to you through my writing and my rituals. And look what you did to me." I wanted to scream and shout but the windows were open. Instead, I lay down on the floor and moaned.

In the silence that followed, I heard Her say, *"I did not abandon you. Who do you think led you to Paliani? You were so angry with me that I had to disguise myself for you to find me. But you did find me there. Do you remember your prayer? You asked for what you believed I had taken from you. You knew I was there. I did not ever abandon you. The path you are on now will not be easy, but I will be with you all the way."*

Everyone Is Waiting

*I*n Lesbos, I felt the island's beauty seducing me as the taxi travelled up the winding mountain roads through the pine forests, and down again through olive groves to the Gulf of Kalloni. As we drove through the marshland at the edge of the sea, I asked the driver to turn down the unmarked dirt road leading to Aphrodite's temple. We passed small farms and crossed the stream created by the spring. Finding the gate of the temple locked, I scaled the fence and lodged a silver ring, two snakes entwined, between the ancient stones, acknowledging the gift Aphrodite had given me.

As we continued on to Mithymna, passing through the outskirts of the town of Kalloni, and climbing back into the mountains, I thought of the friends I had when I lived in Lesbos. Our connections had seemed strong; then they ended. No answers to my letters or telephone calls. I felt my friends didn't really care about me. When I thought of the other townspeople, I felt shame. "Everyone knows I ran after a man who left me," I thought, "and now they will feel sorry for me." I felt sick. The taxi descended again into olive groves, and then the rock of Petra, with its tiny white church clinging to the summit, emerged against the sea. In a few short minutes, Mithymna's hill came into view, crowned by the castle. The taxi deposited me at a hotel just outside the village.

Karin, who greeted me when I arrived, asked if I would like to join her for a late-afternoon swim. As we floated in the embrace of the grey-blue sea, Karin told me that the group I was to address had become fragmented. "There is a great deal of anger," she said. I spoke of similar problems in Ellen's groups. "Some of it is fear that being in the unfamiliar territory of a foreign country will cause you to lose control," I suggested. As we swam farther and farther out, I told Karin the story of my descent into the Skoteino Cave. "I sense your life changing as we speak," Karen said.

I was relieved that Karin suggested we go shopping together before meeting some of the others for dinner. I would not have to face the town alone. At the edge of the village, we ran into a man about my age, once stunningly handsome, who had been one of the town playboys. Now he was walking with his little child, developing a paunch, and beginning to bald. I am not the only one who is getting older, I thought to myself. He greeted me with genuine warmth, introduced his daughter, and asked why I had been gone so long. As Karin and I walked through the narrow streets of the marketplace, this scene was repeated. Shop owners ran out of their shops to greet me. "Where have you been?" they asked. "Why have you forgotten us?" And, "You look more beautiful than ever."

The black-clad widow Maritsa put the gift I was receiving into words when she hugged me outside the tiny hut from which she sells cigarettes, candy, and postcards. "Karolina," she said, "you never did any harm to anyone here. Everyone loves you. Everyone is waiting for you to come back."

When I returned to Athens, I thought I had developed a cold. Then I realized clear water was dripping from my nose. I was releasing tears.

Forgiveness

While walking through the old part of Athens known as the Plaka on a summer day, I heard my name called out, and turned to see Andreas. I felt I like I was seeing a ghost. Nervous and intense, he pulled me away from my friend, and said he needed to speak with me. When we met a few days later, he told me that he had been in a drug rehabilitation community for a year and a half. Upon his release he looked for me because he wanted to apologize for his behavior, but I had moved. "After I left the community," he said, "there were only a few people I wanted to see. You were one of them. I wanted to tell you that I know you only gave me love, care, and help, while I gave you very little in return. *You didn't fail. I failed. I am sorry.*" I was stunned. Andreas had once told me he had a drug problem, but insisted it was in the past. Now, everything fell into place. I accepted his apology, and after sharing our stories, we parted. In the evening, I called Melpo, telling her that I had been crying all afternoon. "You don't sound sad," she responded, "I think you are releasing something."

In the next days, I remembered that Charis had told me that the despair I felt was not about Andreas. I began to see that I had woven a tale with threads of self-judgment, guilt, and rejection, similar to the one I had created about my friends in Mithymna that simply was not true. I had not failed. He had. The only failure I could justly attribute to myself was not seeing that Andreas lied to me about taking drugs. I could forgive myself for not seeing through his lies. I didn't know the physical signs of drug abuse. I didn't know that drug addicts are habitual liars. If I had been able to say when he left, "I didn't fail, he did," I would not have suffered so intensely. I could have moved on with my life.

The fact that I wasn't able to do that had nothing to do with Andreas, and everything to do with me. I had been severely traumatized as a child. Whatever had happened to me back then, I had been wounded so deeply that I did not want to go on living. The feeling of abandonment stemming from that trauma was easily triggered in intimate relationships. I did not know, and perhaps would never know, exactly what event or series of events caused the child I once was to want to die. But I now held the thread that could unweave the cloak of pain and disappointment that had cast a deep shadow over my life. I could stop letting pain that had nothing to do with present realities rule my life.

After my crying had run its course, I added two pictures to my altar. One was of me in a white dress, taken by Andreas, on a night when I was radiantly happy and in love. The other was of the rose gold sea at sunset in Lesbos. Along with the Snake Goddesses, the icon of the Panagia, and the photographs of my mother and grandmother, these images would remind me of the grace and beauty of life. I knew that one day soon, I would be able to look at them without longing or recrimination.

Part Three

PILGRIMAGE

And their feet move

Rhythmically, as tender
feet of Cretan girls
danced once . . .[20]

Groundwork

*I*n the fall, I was ready to lead the Goddess Pilgrimage to Crete I had been anticipating for a full year. I looked forward to introducing thirteen women to the mysteries I had discovered. I did not know that the pilgrimage would be deeply transformative for me as well.

In choosing to travel to Crete, we were seeking to experience a culture in which women could walk bare-breasted, proud of our bodies, without fear of violation. When I told the owner of a jewelry shop in Crete that we were a group of women searching for the ancient Goddess of Crete, she raised her arms as if holding writhing serpents, then cupped her breasts and exclaimed, "Oh, you mean the Goddess with the snakes? She was the first feminist!" "Exactly!" I replied. We were searching for a power that would take root in our bodies, a deeply female and spiritual power.

The culture of ancient Crete was very different from our own. As Lucy Goodison has written, in ancient Crete "we find a society which was in many ways unusual: where women predominated in religious and perhaps social life, where some settlements seem to have been communal, and where there is surprisingly little evidence of military weapons and fortifications."[21] Patterns of dominance were introduced into Crete by Mycenaean warriors from the mainland, who had settled into fortresses in the Peloponnese by 1600 B.C.E. Even though the ancient Cretans built large structures wrongly named "palaces," there is no evidence that kings lived in them from c. 1900 B.C.E, when they were built, to c.1450 B.C.E., when they were destroyed.[22] Most likely these buildings were Sacred Centers, communal gathering places where rituals of the agricultural cycle were celebrated and where planting, harvesting, and trading were organized.

The ancient Cretans venerated the Goddess as the source of life, movement, and beauty, and as Jacquetta Hawkes writes, they celebrated "the grace of life" in their art and their lives.[23] While the Goddess is at the center and women are the primary actors in many of the rituals depicted on seal rings and other artifacts, men are never portrayed as servile or subordinate. It appears that both men and women took delight in their bodies and came together without the specters of fear and self-loathing, dominance and contempt that have marred the relations between the sexes throughout recorded history.

Lacking models for genuine equality between the sexes, some have imagined that ancient Crete was a matriarchy where women ruled over men and may even have sacrificed them. But there is no evidence of this. Habits of dominance and control are the product of militaristic societies, and there are no images of armies or warrior kings in ancient Crete. Why is it so hard for us to imagine a society without dominance? Is it because we long for it, but do not believe we can achieve it? Is it because the very idea that such a society could have existed calls into question patterns of behavior and social organization we have been taught to think are normal and inevitable? Is it because we cannot bear to think that we do not live in the most civilized and evolved culture that has ever existed on our planet? Is it because we are afraid to face the pain that living with violence and the fear of violence has etched into our bodies and our souls?

The vision of a world where dominance and control are not the norm, threatens to open wounds in all of us. The women on the pilgrimage would be hoping to experience the joy of new vision, but might not be prepared for the pain that gives it birth. I was afraid they would be disappointed if the Goddess did not appear to them in living color on the first day of the tour. I had learned that the Goddess is to be found in "the rocks" of Crete. I knew that revelations would come when least expected, and might not be understood until weeks or even months after the tour had ended. It would be important to stay grounded, to find and feel the bedrock that supports and sustains life, throughout our journey.

Living in Greece had made me keenly aware that North Americans approach life with a desire for control. In contrast, Greeks often shrug their shoulders and throw up their hands, saying, *"Ti na kano?"* "What can I do?" Though this attitude has its own problems, it expresses a healthy dose of realism. We cannot control all of the factors that shape our daily lives, let alone our destiny or fate. I hoped that the women on the tour would be willing to give up expectations and to be patient, to wait, and to listen. I had learned that when we expect nothing, much is given.

My friend Carol Lee Sanchez, whose ancestors come from the Laguna Pueblos of New Mexico, once said to me: "You white women know how to raise energy, but you don't know how to ground it. We Indian women ground energy naturally because we are part of the land. I get tired trying to ground it for all of you." I was standing outside a ritual circle where energy was being raised with Carol because I had a headache. I vowed never again to raise energy I could not ground. I felt that my most important task as leader of the pilgrimage would be to help the others to stay grounded.

With this in mind, I decided to place the gesture of pouring libations of milk and honey, water and wine, on altars connected to the earth at the center of our rituals. Offering libations to the Source of Life is one of the most ancient of all sacred acts. Beginning there would connect us in the earth.

Best Laid Plans

*A*s I was about to leave for Crete I was forced—against my will—to relearn the lesson about control I was eager to impart to the group. The day before I was to leave for Crete, my therapy group met. I felt very proud of myself because everything seemed to be falling into place for the tour. There were only a few more details to take care of: I would finish packing in the morning; leave the house at midday; hail a cab; pick up the permit for speaking on the archaeological sites; collect our return ferry tickets from our Greek travel agent, Rena; hail another cab; and arrive at the airport in time to catch my plane. I would confirm trip details by phone after arriving in Crete and share a meal at the home of Cretan friends in the evening. The next morning, I would visit the archaeological museum to refresh my memory; in the late afternoon, I would meet the tour participants at our hotel.

I told the therapy group I was feeling really good about my life. I said I was grateful for the lessons I had learned in the group over the summer and felt my life was changing. Charis looked skeptical. One of the women said she thought there was something false in what I said: I seemed to be trying too hard. There was a long silence. No one came to my defense. I felt like I had been punched in the stomach. I started to cry uncontrollably. The group gathered around me to comfort me, but I felt nothing. When I returned home, the voice I was still struggling to hold back came forth again. *"No one understands you, no one loves you,"* it insisted. I knew this was not true, but I could not stop crying. This time I was not crying tears of release, but tears of despair that came from the well of ancient pain. I tried to tell myself that I had no reason to cry, but I couldn't stop.

That night, I sobbed myself to sleep and began crying again as soon as I woke up. I packed in a daze, certain I would forget something important, and wondered if I would still be crying when the group arrived the next day. I closed my bags just in time to hail a taxi to take me downtown. Rena was waiting for me in front of the office that had prepared my permit, and waited while I went upstairs. Then she handed me the tickets and embraced me warmly—predicting that the tour would be a great success. She left me standing on a street corner, assuring me that there was plenty of time to make my plane.

But I didn't find a cab. A pre-election bomb had gone off at the central bus depot the night before, and people were afraid to take the buses. All the taxis that passed me had passengers and none was going to the airport. After standing for forty-five minutes with my arm stretched out, I realized I was going to miss my plane. I called Rena, who checked with the airport and informed me that due to the upcoming elections, all flights were full for the next ten days. By that time I was sobbing hysterically in the phone booth. Rena had suggested the ferryboat, but I knew that I would not be able to sleep even if I secured a cabin, because I am claustrophobic.

Rena arrived on her motorbike to take me and my bags to a street where I could find a taxi to Piraeus, the port of Athens. I was crying that I didn't want to go on the ferry, but Rena insisted, hailed the taxi, and pushed me and my bags into it. The taxi driver could see that I was upset. He called the airport to see if there was any way I could make my plane and then tried to cheer me up on the drive to the port. When we arrived, he stopped the cab, and went into the ferry office with me to make sure I would be able to get a first-class cabin. I thanked him profusely, wondering if he had been sent by the Goddess.

I managed to control my tears while climbing the narrow staircase of the boat. My cabin was larger than expected, with three beds. If I was alone in the room, I might be able to sleep. I checked later and saw that no baggage had been deposited on either of the two bunk beds. After dinner, I found two other women in the cabin. Slamming the door in frustration, I collapsed in tears in the hallway. If I could not sleep, how could I regain the control I would need to guide the other women on a Goddess Pilgrimage to Crete?

Help Abounding

I slept fitfully on a couch in the first class lounge of the ferryboat. When I disembarked, bleary-eyed, very early in the morning, I was surprised to see my Cretan friends, Maria and Giorgos, waiting for me with their car. I had asked Rena to cancel my dinner with them the previous evening, and I didn't expect to see them until after the tour. I have never been happier to see anyone, anywhere.

Giorgos lifted my bags into the trunk of the car, and Maria announced that we were going "home" for a big breakfast. Maria sat me down at the kitchen table in their modest apartment, while she moved gracefully around the kitchen, chatting, making coffee, setting out bread, butter, and homemade jam. "Did you notice I have lost another ten pounds," she said coquettishly, her hands on her hips, her dark eyes flashing. "I'm jealous," I teased. Her husband Giorgos asked with genuine warmth how I had been since I last saw them. Soon we were joined by their tall, awkward, good-looking son, who also seemed happy to see me.

After breakfast, Maria took charge as we walked into town to do the things I had to do: find a pair of walking shoes, as I had forgotten to pack the ones I bought for the trip; buy an extra copy of the guidebook I would give to the participants; check with the travel agency in Crete about the bus we were expecting the next day; arrange dinner for the group at a local restaurant; purchase candles for the caves; stock up on supplies for my period which had just begun; and finally, check in at our hotel. I don't think I could have managed without Maria. Luckily she likes to shop. We accomplished all of the tasks, and even found time to stop for *loukoumades*, honey-drenched Greek donut holes.

Maria put a fresh leg of goat on the stove before we left, and it was ready when we returned. "You can stay with us any time," Giorgos said as we finished a hearty lunch. "You are one of ours now." I knew this was an important statement in a culture that makes a strong distinction between "family" and "strangers," a term used for everyone who is not family. Though I was exhausted when I lay down on the bed in my hotel room in the early afternoon, I had stopped crying. I had not done everything I intended to do, but I had done everything I needed to do.

The group arrived in the late afternoon. When we introduced ourselves before dinner, I was pleased to discover that most of the women were about my age, with a few younger and a few older. They seemed eager and excited to begin our journey together. The restaurant Maria and I selected in the morning was a great success. The waiters brought us small plates brimming with cold octopus vinaigrette, mussels in tomato sauce, little meatballs, fava bean dip, boiled greens, salad with feta cheese, tiny olives, tzatziki, fried potatoes, and golden retsina, all served family style. Tired and full of good food, most of the women said goodnight early, but several of us lingered over the raki.

Language of the Goddess

ecause I had not been able to visit the Heraklion Archaeological Museum before the tour, I did not have everything "under control" when we visited it the next day. The museum was being painted and the signs, such as "Neolithic and Pre-Palace Finds" and "Palace of Knossos" were not in place.[24] Even though I had visited the museum several times and felt I knew the artifacts fairly well, I was forced to open the guidebook to refresh my memory. I was embarrassed because I thought I should know "everything." Later, several of the women told me that my not knowing every date and detail allowed them to understand that the really important things they would learn on the trip were not those that could be memorized or learned from a book.

The museum was our introduction to the culture of ancient Crete. The others gathered close as I pointed out the small Neolithic Goddess figures in the first room. I explained that because women were the most likely inventors of agriculture, pottery, and weaving in the Neolithic era, these images were not mere "fertility figurines." They represented the social and cultural power of women at the time. The ability of women to give birth is an awesome power, but it was not the only power women had: they also "gave birth" to plants, pots, and woven cloth. As potters, women may have been the creators of many of the objects on display.

One of my favorite images is a small ceramic jug in the shape of a woman with narrow snakelike arms, her body decorated with double triangles and squiggly lines, who holds a water pitcher. According to Marija Gimbutas, all of the symbols on the objects we were seeing had meaning, and could be "read" as part of the "language of the Goddess." The double triangles might symbolize the planting knowledge of women passed down from mother to daughter, and the curving lines the energy of growing plants. Could women have used jugs like these to water the first planted seeds? As the earth is the body of the Goddess, the combination of human, animal, plant, and elemental forms expresses Her cosmic power.[25]

The offerings left at mountaintop shrines include images of male and female worshippers, the women barebreasted with long skirts, and the men wearing only cinch belts and codpieces. There is no suggestion in these images that one sex gazed on the body of the other as an object;

rather they seem to express equality and mutual delight. The image of three black birds resting on three columns is interpreted as an "epiphany" of the Goddess, an idea that continues up through the appearance of the Holy Spirit in the form of the dove. As we continued our journey through the museum, the women began to recognize a continuity of symbolism. Spirals were everywhere, as were dots representing seeds, and triangles symbolizing the vulva.

We were delighted to discover the Snake Goddesses in the fourth room. Though we had been taught that the Woman and the Snake were the source of Evil, we were beginning to see that once the Woman and the Snake were Sacred. I said that I imagined that the Snake Goddesses were placed together on low altars in the Sacred Centers, with people entering the small dark rooms and leaving offerings, much as contemporary Cretans enter small churches to light candles to the Panagia and the saints. I suggested that women dressed like the Snake Goddesses would have performed rituals in these small rooms.

Near the Snake Goddesses are two small plaques of nursing animals, a cow and a goat, both with very long horns. Though archaeologists and others like to identify horned animals with "the male principle," these images prove them wrong. Where the sex is not clearly indicated, horned animals can be either male or female. Even the much-reproduced image of the "Bull's Head Rhyton," a pouring vessel carved from black stone with inset rock crystal eyes, could be a cow. If so, the milk of nurture, not the blood of sacrifice, might have been poured from the opening of its mouth.

When we reached the room with three larger than life-size bronze labryses (often called "double axes"), we stared in awe. A symbol found in Neolithic Anatolia, the labyris may originally have been created by doubling the female sacred triangle. In its more stylized form, it echoes the ritual gestures of women with up-raised arms, the wings of birds and butterflies, and the phases of the moon. The labyris was never held by men or used for performing blood sacrifice. As I was explaining the meaning of the symbol, Jana and her friend Karen, claimed the spaces between the labryses, where they stood facing us with raised arms, embodying the gestures ancient priestesses. Visiting the museum was a learning experience that was seeping from our minds into our bodies.

Ritual at Knossos

*M*y discomfort that I did not know everything was intensified when we visited the archaeological site known as the "Palace" of Knossos in the afternoon. A labyrinthine complex of many rooms, it was excavated and rebuilt by the British archaeologist Sir Arthur Evans, who developed the first theories about the religion and culture of ancient Crete. As I had only been granted permission to speak on the archaeological sites a few days before the tour began, I had not memorized the maps of this complex site. There was no way I could name or explain the use of every individual part of the architectural structure, so I was forced to use a guidebook again. The group didn't seem to mind discovering the site together, and as I relaxed, I realized that I had many insights to share that were not included in the guidebook.

Evans, an aristocratic gentleman who favored white linen suits, believed that he had discovered a king's palace. He named the culture he was unearthing "Minoan," after the legendary "King Minos," mentioned in the *Iliad* of Homer. If there ever was a King Minos, he lived at the time of the Trojan War, and he represented the Mycenaean rulers who had destroyed the mis-named "Minoan" culture several centuries earlier. Archaeologist Nanno Marinatos argues that the "Palaces" of ancient Crete were not royal residences but religious and administrative centers: combining the functions of a church, a social hall, a farmer's co-operative, and a town hall.[26] These functions were not separate as they are today, for the Goddess presided over the rituals of the agricultural year: people came together at festival times to sing and dance in honor of Her. Distribution systems and record-keeping ensured that a portion of the harvest was set aside for festivals, and that the rest was shared fairly. Seedtime called for rituals to bless the seeds and plant them with reverence and respect for the earth and its cycles of birth, death, and regeneration. Harvest was the time to thank the Goddess for the fruits and vegetables that spring forth from bounteous earth. Building on Marinatos' ideas, I renamed the "Palaces" "Sacred Centers."

Failing to find any image of a "King" at Knossos, Evans constructed a figure he called the "Prince of the Lilies" from fragments of frescoes. He imagined him to be a priest-king who ruled Knossos from the Throne Room at Knossos. This reconstruction has been disputed: the crown Evans placed on the head of his Prince may belong to a mythical creature called a griffon. Nanno Marinatos believes that the Throne Room is part of a shrine complex designed for a ritual drama involving the epiphany, or appearance, of the Goddess. The Goddess, in the form of the priestess who embodied Her, sat on the throne, and the griffons wearing elaborate crowns were Her companion animals.

We began our tour in the West Court, a paved area outside the main building complex. Here, Processional Paths, a common feature of the architecture of ancient Crete, lead to altars where offerings were placed. The raised pathways mark "the way" of the rituals to the Goddess. At the edge of the court are three large stone-lined pits, which may have been granaries for the storage of grain to bake bread for the festivals. Storage of grain, wine, and oil was later moved inside the building complex.

Placing our feet on stones where the feet of "young Cretan girls" once walked, we were led to the North Entrance. There, Evans placed a seven-foot tall carved stone image known as the Horns of Consecration, situating it to frame Sacred Mount Juctas.[27] Several of the women felt the irresistible urge to stand in front of the horns with upraised arms—as I had done on my first visit to Knossos. Like all ancient symbols, the Horns of Consecration has many meanings: it may refer to the horns of animals; to the curves of mountain peaks and valleys; as well as to the upraised arms of the priestesses. From where we stood, we could see the large, open, Central Court, where rituals, dances, and dramas were performed. In the miniature fresco we had seen a few hours earlier, women in yellow and blue dresses danced in the court. Closing our eyes we could almost see them. Continuing on to the Throne Room, we visualized the priestess dressed as the Snake Goddess, emerging through a doorway to take her seat on the throne.

For many of us, this was enough, but Sue was eager to find the Theatral Area, a wide stepped platform approached by Processional Paths. Sue took charge of the guidebook and led the way. She told us that she had read that the people taking part in ritual processions stopped at the Theatral Area to watch a sacred drama. As some of us tried to imagine this, others went to the pathway leading up the steps. Led by Jana, they raised their arms and followed the Processional Path. We all joined them, processing up the stairs and on to the South Entrance. The ritual had begun without anyone planning it.[28] Reaching the Sacred Court again, we dispersed to meditate.

Arriving back at the bus before the others, I slipped across the street to a tourist shop. There I bought a small copy of the seated Neolithic Goddess with beaked face, thick snakelike limbs, and water lines decorating Her body that we had seen in the museum.[29] This early Goddess would grace all of our altars during the pilgrimage. Soon we would be affectionately calling Her "the Tour Goddess."

Tree of Life

*T*he next day we visited the Panagia Myrtia, the Sacred Myrtle Tree, at the convent of Paliani. I explained that the adoration given to the holy tree is a living testimony to the survival of the ancient worship of the Tree of Life. A gold ring in the Heraklion Museum depicts women tending sacred trees while the Goddess appears in their midst. Through the nuns who create a beautiful garden for the Panagia of their Holy Tree, we are given a glimpse of ancient priestesses creating gardens for the Goddess and the Tree of Life.

As I retold the story of how the icon wanted to be worshipped in the myrtle tree, I shared my feeling that the Goddess could be found in the images and icons of the Panagia and the female saints. When Christianity prohibited the worship of the Goddess, the people were not deterred. They continued to worship Her as they had always done. I said that we could think of the Panagia of the Sacred Myrtle Tree as a bridge linking us not only to the ancient past, but to the faith of all the women throughout the centuries who shared their hopes, dreams, and prayers in this holy place. "*Pan-Agia*," I continued, "does not mean 'Virgin Mary,' but rather 'All Holy' in the feminine gender. This name could have been— and most probably was—used for the Goddess. The *Pan-Agia Myrtia*, the All Holy Myrtle Tree, must also be a name that predates Christianity." I added that the Christian Orthodox Church believes in the "real presence" of the saints and the divinity in the icons, much as the Roman Catholic Church believes in the "real presence" of Christ in the body and blood of Communion. Thus Greeks touch and kiss the icons feeling as close to them as they once did to their own mother's breasts.

As I looked around the convent garden, I recognized its similarity to the Sacred Center at Knossos. It too had an open court, enclosed by a series of small rooms. At Paliani, the ritual focus was at the tree at the far end of the courtyard and in the church that had been built in front of it. The miniature frescoes in the Heraklion Museum show that a tree or trees were planted in the Central Court at Knossos too. Like Knossos, Paliani is surrounded by productive fields. As at Knossos, local people gather at Paliani on festival days. Both Paliani and Knossos are Sacred Centers in the heart of the surrounding communities.

For the ritual at the Sacred Tree, I asked each pilgrim to take one of the ribbons I brought, without consciously choosing a color. We would meditate on the significance of the color that had chosen us, and then tie the ribbon onto the tree with a prayer or a wish. I hoped the deep dusky rose ribbon, that I felt symbolized Aphrodite, would find me, but instead I received a sky blue ribbon. At the Sacred Tree, without having planned to do so in advance, I shared stories of my experiences with the Panagia Myrtia. I spoke of how my disappointment in love provoked my loss of faith in myself, in my writing, and in the Goddess; of the healing I found at the tree and in the church; and of the revelation that She had not abandoned me, that came after I expressed my anger. I felt exposed and vulnerable and was not sure how the others would respond. When I looked around the circle, I could see that most of others had tears in their eyes. Sharing what had seemed to be the most personal and in that sense, isolating, of stories, I found that I was not alone.

Standing before the tree with the light blue ribbon in my hand, I remembered that I had purchased a bright blue bead, protection against the evil eye, the previous day. In many cultures, blue, the color of the sky, is thought to be the color of protection. In rural Greece, people pin a blue eye to a baby's clothing when it is taken outside the protection of its home. I found the bead in my bag, tied it to the ribbon, and asked the Goddess for protection on the journey that was beginning to unfold.

After tying our ribbons to the tree—others too had added gifts—we gathered under its branches. Each of us shared the meaning of the ribbon she had received, while an aged nun looked on from a balcony above. Robin asked if she could sing. It felt right that she do so. Then we grounded the energy by touching the tree. One woman was sobbing and several others seemed to be clinging to the tree for dear life. It was with great reluctance that we said goodbye. The next day, several of the women told me that if the pilgrimage had ended at Paliani, it would have been enough.

Taste the Sweetness

*L*eaving the convent, our bus climbed into the Psiloritis Mountains en route to Zaros. My body tensed in anticipation as I thought of hiking the gorge, the raki festival, and haunting sounds of the Cretan lyra. When we arrived, I felt calmed by the sound of rushing water flowing under the mill which was next to the tavern where I chose the salmon trout.

Though I was tired, I could not rest after lunch. The mountains called. I allowed Patricia, who seemed at home on the path, to take the lead. I was delighted to see confidence and determination in her gait as her long legs took control of the trail. Letting her go first gave me the chance to relax and absorb the healing strength of the mountains rising steeply on each side of the gorge.

The next morning we travelled down the mountain to Phaistos. The "Sacred Center" is situated on the top of a hill in the middle of a richly cultivated valley. The ancient stones were bathed in the clear light of October in Greece. The Kamares Cave, a destination for pilgrims in ancient times, is visible as a black smudge on one of the twin peaks or double breasts of Sacred Mount Ida. It was there that the first examples of the delicate black, red, and ochre pottery known as Kamares Ware were found.

Once inside the archaeological site, which had not been as much reconstructed as Knossos, we began to recognize familiar features: raised Processional Paths cutting across an open court outside the building complex; a stepped Theatral Area; large circular granaries; and of course, the open Central Court. Images from the Heraklion Museum came to life as we imagined bare-breasted women in long flounced skirts and men wearing only belts and loin cloths walking on Processional Paths carrying Kamares Ware pitchers and bowls laden with offerings of the first fruits of the harvest.

We were forced to open the guidebook to locate the shrine rooms to the west of the court. Though I still wished I knew more, the group did not mind reading again from the guidebook. I was beginning to relax: everything was working out "just fine," even though I did not know everything. In time we came to the exquisite reconstructed rooms lined with alabaster slabs. Because this area is so beautiful, the archaeologists called it the Private Quarters of the King and Queen. Being more attuned to beauty, the Queen was given the room with a series of doors that could be opened to take in a breath-taking view. Challenging this conventional interpretation, Marinatos identified the rooms as part of a Shrine. Directly across from them was the Treasury where sacred items were stored in large stationary "chests." There, the mysterious Phaistos Disk, inscribed with an undeciphered hieroglyphic script was found. Like the Snake Goddesses, it must have been taken out on festival days to be displayed on one of the low benches in the shrine rooms. Perhaps the disk had been carried with much pomp and ceremony down the stairs that separated the shrine rooms.

Our next stop was Agia Triada, a "summer residence" or small Sacred Center not far from Phaistos. There we found a Mycenaean shrine consisting of two small square rooms with a long bench at the back of the inner room. Finding ourselves alone on the site, we inaugurated what would become our pilgrimage ritual tradition. We placed small terra cotta pitchers, tiny hand-sewn triangles filled with myrtle leaves from Paliani, our jewelry, and the copy of the small Neolithic Goddess I found at Knossos on the altar bench. First we poured milk that nurtures human and animal babies; then honey, sweet gift of the bees; then water, the source of life; and finally, wine, loosener of limbs and spirits. As the liquid poured from the vessels in our hands into the worn places in the rocks, we sensed that we were returning the gifts we had been given to their Source. Our gestures were hesitant and much was left unspoken, but still, we felt our connection to ancient women who had performed similar rituals in this very place. Finally, we offered each other honey from a copy of a Kamares Ware cup decorated with spirals and flowers, repeating "Taste the sweetness of life." Robin led us in song, and we ended the ritual in a tight embrace. We grounded the energy by placing our hands on the altar. Some of us tucked our sacred objects into crevices in the stones, while others removed them, now blessed, to place on other altars.

During the ritual one of the women became concerned that the guard was watching. But he neither approached us nor said anything.[30] As our journey continued, other men would stand, respectfully, just outside our ritual circle. I was learning that men can accept, appreciate, and even be present at women's mysteries, just as Naomi and I had been present at the men's mystery of distilling raki.

Music in Zaros

Back in Zaros, a night of Cretan music and dancing awaited us. I hoped to share some of the magic of the raki festival with the group. Kostas, the lyra player, and Giannis, the young boy would play for us, while Nikos and Themis would invite young men from the village to dance with us. We were joined by the sweet, round-eyed young woman who was the receptionist at our hotel.

The evening did not begin as planned. Kostas, who wore his regular clothes at the raki party, arrived in his best traditional Cretan black shirt and high black boots, with a microphone and amplifier. I feared that he was going to "perform for the tourists," rather than sing from his heart. The taverna owner, who had promised to negotiate a fair price, had forgotten to do so, and Kostas was asking four times his standard fee. After a bit of shouting that probably was not appreciated by the group, we reached an uneasy compromise. I thought Kostas was taking advantage of for-eigners, and I worried that he would be angry because I had not agreed to pay the fee he asked.

All of that was forgotten when the music started. Kostas was in good form. Everyone was entranced by the unfamil-iar strains of the *mantinadas*. Nikos pulled us all up to learn a simple dance called the *sigano*, and with my arm on his shoulder, I was not able to hide somewhere in the middle of the line. As I am right-left dyslexic, I have difficulty learning steps, but on this night my body seemed to move effortlessly with the rhythms of the music. Four men arrived with their instruments and joined the band—simply because they wanted to have a good time. The music flowed. Wine and raki flowed. We danced on and on, now in a circle, now in a line, snaking between the tables. Even though most of the men were younger than we were, they seemed to have a frank and open appreciation of our femaleness, combined with a playfulness and gentle insistence that they would be hon-ored if one of us said "yes." A few of the men took the mi-crophone to sing *mantinadas* to "that beautiful foreign woman who turns away from me." There a few kisses and several close, slow dances at the end of the evening, but as far as I know, nothing more. In the morning all of us were smil-ing. We had a good time, but it was more than that. Through the music, our spirits had come into our bodies, and in the dance each of us felt proud to be a woman.

Letting Go

$\mathcal{L}$eaving Zaros, we drove through the mountains to Archanes, where we would visit the shrine on the top of Mount Juctas, the Sacred Mountain we had seen from the Horns of Consecration at Knossos. I had called the guard who said he would open the gate for us, without answer. When we arrived at the small Archanes Museum, we were told that the guard had gone home to vote, taking the key with him. Frustrated by factors beyond my control, I started to fall apart. "But he promised to take us to the mountain," I screamed. I was sent to the cafe where the guard was known to spend his free time. Maybe he had not left yet. The woman behind the bar and several old men tried to calm the tall blonde who was shouting at them in Greek by calling the mayor. He informed me that the guard did not work for him, but then, just as I was about to scream at him too, he remembered that an archaeologist was excavating the site as we spoke. He assured me that she would let us inside.

Mountain Shrines, or as they are usually called, Peak Shrines, were situated near towns and villages, and Sacred Mountains were visible from all of the Sacred Centers. The path to the top of Mount Juctas would have been steep, but it would have taken only an hour or two to walk up from Archanes, no more than three from Knossos. Those who lived near the mountains would have been used to walking in them to collect herbs and greens and to tend their flocks. Before automobiles became common, the people of Archanes climbed the mountain on foot in midsummer as their ancestors must have done; the festival is now known as the Metamorphosis or Transfiguration of Christ, and is celebrated in a church situated on one of Juctas's two high peaks. The walk to Juctas would have required effort, but it would not have been difficult for any but the very young and the very old.

Our bus took us with difficulty up a winding dirt road up to the new stone path near the summit that we would follow to the top. We elected to walk in silence to appreciate the view of farmlands that dotted the valley below, stretching all the way to the sea. Our bus driver, Giannis, ran ahead of us, and when we arrived he was speaking animatedly with the archaeologist. A few minutes later, he informed me that she was a friend of his, because he had excavated on the site.

He explained that after heroic efforts on his part, she had agreed to interrupt her work to speak to us.

As she stood on the rock outcropping of the peak, Alexandra Karetsou's short sturdy legs seemed to be rooted in the mountain. She spoke hesitantly and very seriously at first, citing authorities to back up every claim. But as she sensed that we were following her with our bodies and spirits as well as our minds, she began to smile shyly and speak freely. She told us that this mountaintop was selected for the shrine, not only because it is the highest peak in proximity to Knossos and Archanes, but also because in the rock there is a gaping hole, an opening to the depths of earth. The deity worshipped was most definitely the Goddess, and probably by Mycenaean times, also the Cretan Zeus. "But the Cretan Zeus," she insisted, "was a young, unbearded youth, who had nothing to do with the old man with the thunderbolts worshipped by the Greeks."

The offerings retrieved from the crevice ranged from simple terracotta images of sheep and goats to richly decorated pottery and stone offering tables decorated with Linear A. The pilgrims came from all walks of life, and offerings of arms and legs suggested that they prayed not only for their flocks, but also for their own health and healing. Karetsou confided that she found small images of women giving birth, but that with the exception of the eminent Professor Platon, the other archaeologist refused to recognize them as such. "So," she said with a sigh, "when I discuss them I have to say, 'Professor Platon has identified them as images of women giving birth.'" Taking advantage of the opening she had created, I decided to tell her about the pilgrimage and our search for images of female power. "There are many women like us in America, eagerly awaiting the work of women like you," I said in conclusion, "I wonder what new interpretations might come forth if women archaeologists, instead of laboring to prove the obvious, could speculate as freely as male archaeologists always have been able to do."

Karetsou led us to the crevice. I must have imagined it to be a small hole, because I was surprised to find myself gazing down into a deep crack in the rock that looked an entrance to a cave. "Do you think the people climbed down into the crevice?" I wondered aloud. "I don't think so," Karetsou replied. "Our workers have been able to descend with difficulty and only with ropes. We have excavated to a depth of thirteen meters. The crevice was full of offerings; we have not gotten to the bottom yet, but we will probably have to stop, because of the danger." I asked if we could pour libations into the offering. "Pour anything you like," she responded, "and throw offerings in too if you want."[31]

I remembered the gaudy sequined red brocade "sacred heart" that had caught my eye at Paliani. I found it in my bag and cast it into the crevice, asking the Goddess to heal my broken heart and all the ancient pain it carried. It stuck on a ledge. I wanted it to fall all the way down, so I poured water on it, and it continued its journey. As I stared into the opening in the earth, I realized that with the winter rains the cardboard frame of heart would dissolve into the elements: some years later the fabric too would disintegrate, leaving only the sequins. That was a comforting thought. Inspired by the promise of freedom, I went to the highest place on the Sacred Mountain, raising my arms priestess style. Then I began to turn slowly, taking in the view, singing, "I circle around, I circle around, the boundaries of the earth."[32]

Earth Mother

The Skoteino Cave was the next destination on the pilgrimage, but first we would stop in the village where Christina had promised to cook a special lunch for us. A sweet-faced woman in her fifties, Christina owns one of the town's two small *cafeneons*, and usually only serves appetizers to accompany the raki she serves to the old men. Like the Venus of Willendorf, she has slender arms that rest often on her full breasts and belly.

When we arrived, the table was not set. Had she forgotten us? I was reassured that she most certainly had not. While we set the tables with the glasses and plates that we found in the dish rack, Christina appeared with plates of fried potatoes and tzatziki, followed by tomato and cucumber salads, garnished with feta and tiny olives. I opened the refrigerator and began pulling out bottles of soda and beer. Christina returned bearing a huge shallow pan filled with tiny stuffed grape leaves and squash blossoms, as well as small stuffed tomatoes and peppers. The meal set before us surpassed every expectation, and even though we ate greedily, we were not able to finish it. I suggested that we return to eat again on the way back from the cave.

While we were enjoying our meal, we were joined by Nikos Markakis, known as "the cave man." Tall, quiet, and with thinning white hair and kind blue eyes, Mr. Nikos fell in love with the cave as a young boy. As an adult he had worked with all of the archaeologists and speleologists who explored and documented the cave. He waits on the bench outside his house every day, offering to guide the few tourists who visit the cave. If they pay him, it's fine, and if they don't, he is still happy to have shown them the cave. I met Mr. Nikos the day I descended to the cave on my own. Proud of myself, I stopped in the *cafeneon* to announce what I had accomplished. "Surely you didn't go all the way down on your own," Christina stated. "Let me call the cave man who will tell you how far you got." When I described my descent to Mr. Nikos, he agreed that I had indeed reached the center. Mr. Nikos—I could never address him as Nikos—became my image of ancient Cretan men: gentle and graceful, at home in his body, deeply respectful of women, and fond of repeating, "Man never made anything to compare with what Nature made." I would often say that he was the kindest man I had ever met.

Though I had tried to explain to Mr. Nikos that the women needed to make the journey to the depths of the cave on their own, he had arrived to show us the way. His shy smile and obvious delight in being with us won me over. I didn't have the heart to disappoint him. Mr. Nikos had appeared to remind me that I do not have to do everything myself. As we drove to the cave, I told the story of my solitary descent into the cave the previous spring. The cave is the womb of our Mother Earth, "a place of birth, rebirth, and transformation. Our descent into the Skoteino Cave, I suggested, could catalyze a deep internal shift, a turning point in their lives, as it had in mine.

Before we began our descent, we lit candles to Agia Paraskevi, the patron saint of eyesight, asking her to guide our feet in the cave, and open us to revelation. Mr. Nikos told us that the original church of Agia Paraskevi had been inside the cave, but when a part of the cave collapsed, it was moved to its present position above the cave.

In the first enormous room of the cave, Mr. Nikos showed us a stalagmite that looks like a bear or a dog, guarding the entrance to the lower levels of the cave. Beside it, on a large free-standing rock, he pointed to the naturally formed bas relief that looks like a woman in ancient Cretan dress sitting on a rock. Our eyes still adjusting to the semi-darkness, we struggled to see the woman or Goddess in the naturally formed shapes on the rock, but when we did, we saw all of her children as well.

We lit our candles in preparation for the descent into the darkness. It would have been easy to slip along the way, but Mr. Nikos waited patiently at every turn, offering us a hand to grasp, a shoulder to lean on, and even his foot to step on, as we made our way down. On the second level, he identified a large stalactite as the image of the ancient Cretan Goddess. Below Her was a natural altar, a large flat "table" attached to large stalactite "wall" with patterns and niches formed by flowing water. Next to it is a hole where offerings were thrown. "We know this altar was used by the ancient Cretans," Mr. Nikos told us, "because we excavated carloads of broken pottery from this very place, and found offerings at the bottom of the hole too. We also found two bronze statues of worshipping men, and a couple in a position I hesitate to describe," he added.

It was almost dark in the small room that enclosed the altar, where we placed our candles, the ceramic copy of the Neolithic Goddess I now carried with me, our jewelry, and other offerings. I placed a silver ring, my thank offering for the strength I found in the Skoteino Cave, on the head of my little Goddess, where it sat like a crown. Mr. Nikos and the bus driver stood quietly outside our circle as we poured libations and sang. Milk, honey, water, and wine glistened in the candlelight, as our voices echoed off the walls of the cave.

After we grounded the power with our hands on the altar, I dropped my silver ring into the hole next to the altar. As I heard it fall into the darkness I felt an enormous gratitude.

As we began our descent to the third and fourth levels, the excitement built. I kept running ahead, and Mr. Nikos kept calling me back. I was the first to slide through the final passageway to the center. The large stalactite formation that I remembered was revealed by my candle. I leaned against it and waited for the others. When we were all settled, we extinguished our candles for a silent meditation. I could hear the water dripping within the cave as I prayed for healing. I could feel that Cathleen sitting next to me was shaking. Later she would tell me that energy was coursing through her. We sat in silence for what seemed like a very long time.

When we opened our eyes and lit our candles, Robin moved the beam of her flashlight around the walls of the high-ceilinged room. "Look I see a Goddess," she exclaimed. "And another one," someone else replied. "And over here." "A Mother and a Daughter." "An old woman." We knew that we were not the first to have seen such images in the cave walls.

Soon we began the ascent. Emerging from the womb of the Great Mother, Sue confided, "When I was born my parents wanted a boy. I suffered a lot for that. Now I am glad to be a girl. I feel reborn." We embraced each other whispering, "I'm so glad you are a girl." As the other women reached the mouth of the cave, we hugged each of them in turn, announcing, "It's a girl! I am so glad it's another girl!" We could now imagine what it could have been like to have been born into a culture where mothers were honored and girls were treasured. Layers of shame and self-recrimination slipped off us like the skin of a snake. We were open and vulnerable, but we were becoming whole.

Tired and hungry, we returned to Christina, the mother who would feed and appreciate us. We grabbed our plates and filled them. The radio was playing Greek music, and everyone felt gay. We raised our glasses to Mr. Nikos, who wished that we would all return. We laughed and sang and toasted our courage. When we thought we could eat no more, Christina produced a honey-drenched cake. "They baked cakes to the Queen of Heaven,[33] I cried out as I took the first piece. "Was it really good?" Christina asked coyly. We raised our glasses to toast her.

As we prepared to leave, Christina announced that the drinks from lunch were a gift from Mr. Nikos, while the drinks from our dinner were her gift. The group left almost twice as much as Christina asked for the meal, and would have been happy to have left more. Christina must have gotten a shock when she counted the money, for, just as the bus was about to pull away, she knocked on its door, holding out a large plastic container filled with golden raisins like the ones we had seen drying on raised platforms as we travelled through the countryside. "I can't take this," I said, looking at Giannis. "Oh yes you can," he admonished. During the next days we passed the raisins around the bus whenever we were hungry, and left some as offerings on our altars, but like the proverbial loaves and fishes, there were always more.

Harvest Home

The next day when we arrived at archaeological site of Nirou Hani to meet the guard who would take us to the Eilitheia Cave, my plans were foiled again. The gates were locked, and there was no one there. In a nearby shop, I learned that the new guard had been sick the past few days. Instead of fighting to get my way, I threw up my hands and said, *"Ti na kanoume?"* "What can we do?" I told the group that we would have to "make do" with a long lunch and a refreshing swim, and to my great surprise, no one seemed to mind missing an important cave.

At midday, we arrived at Malia, a Sacred Center built at the edge of the sea. When I looked for the pass that would give us free entrance and allow me to speak, I could not find it anywhere. I had dropped and retrieved it at Knossos and at Phaistos, but I was pretty sure I had not lost it; I thought it was tucked into the guidebook I had forgotten in my hotel room. Carol paid for our tickets without complaint, and the guards allowed me to speak.

Leaving the pass behind made me realize that I was even more tired than I had realized. The trip was going well, but I was still struggling to keep everything "under control." I had not recovered from the loss of sleep on the ferry, and, in addition, I had developed a bad cough. I was on the verge of losing my voice, and sometimes could only speak in a whisper. I knew I was trying to do too much, but I didn't feel I could delegate anything, as I was the one who had planned our itinerary, and I was the only one who could speak Greek. When I told the group how tired I was, Giannis offered to help with the phone calls, and several of the women offered to do what they could—including bringing me water when my voice faltered, and rubbing my shoulders at meals. Carol agreed to become the keeper of the valuable permit.

Earlier in the day, I had stopped a gypsy truck and purchased fruit and vegetables with the idea that we might place them on the large Kernos Stone, a large round offering table with thirty-four circular indentations around its circumference and a larger one at its center.[34] The guards did not follow us around the site or pay any attention to what we were doing. We placed beans, onions, garlic, apples, tomatoes, eggplants, and squash in every carved opening, creating a colorful living mandala. We gave thanks for the wonderful "fruits of the earth" we had been eating at every meal, and for the "spiritual fruits" we were reaping and would continue to reap. This time, rather than singing, we held hands in silence.

Panagia in Chains

$\mathcal{T}$he next day the bus climbed into the mountains where we would visit the Psychro and Trapeza caves. On the way we stopped at the small church of the Panagia Kera Kardiotissa, mainly, I thought, to break up the long bus ride. I did not anticipate that it too would become a site of revelation. The convent is nestled among trees on the side of the mountain. Here is found the icon of the "Panagia in Chains." The story says that the icon was stolen and taken to Constantinople, but returned at night to the monastery, the third time bearing chains and part of the column to which it had been affixed. A little garden surrounds the green column just outside the church, while the icon and its chain are in the church.

We took turns approaching the icon. I was standing with Marian, who like me, had suffered a loss of love. When our turn came, Marian and I were mesmerized by the chain hanging from hooks on the wall near the icon. Marian reached out her hands and gently shook the chain. I imagined that she was praying to be released from the chains that bound her. "I often pray for my true love," I whispered, "but today, I am simply asking for health—mental health would be good." We held the chain together, repeating our prayers with tears in our eyes. The Virgin's eyes expressed an immense sadness that seemed to encompass our pain. I wondered if She too hoped for release from the chains that bound her in a patriarchal world.

A bit later, alone in the garden, looking out to the mountains, I felt a deep peace. New words to the familiar song, "Ancient Mother," formed in my mind:

> Mountain Mother, I hear you calling me.
> Mountain Mother, please hear our cry.
> Mountain Mother, we have come back to you.
> Mountain Mother, we hear your sigh.

There are mountains everywhere in Crete, and I began to suspect that the highest visible mountain was one of the primary images of the Goddess.

Sour Milk

*L*eaving the church, we climbed into the mountain, crossing the line where olive trees can no longer survive, higher and higher. The Dictean Mountain range surrounds the Lasithi Plain, one of the bread baskets of Crete. The Psychro Cave is the legendary place where the Cretan Zeus was hidden away from the father who wanted to kill him, and fed on milk and honey. Long before Zeus came into the picture, the cave was Sacred to the Mountain Mother. Pilgrims must have come to worship Her from near and far, for Mount Dicte is the Sacred Mountain that can be seen from the Sacred Center of Malia.

We accepted the help of a guide to take us down into the cave.[35] Unlike the gentle Mr. Nikos, this wily mountain man had a propensity to let his hands linger on breasts and buttocks as he helped us down a very slippery path—luckily the group took this in stride. A forest of stalagmites and stalactites surrounded us as we descended toward a cold lake at the bottom of the cave. Our guide pointed out the small opening through which the goat and the bee fed the infant Zeus, and then he took us into the small cave within a cave where the baby was hidden. Whatever we made of the story, we recognized this dark, wet cave as a sacred space.[36] But there were too many people coming and going for us to create a ritual there.

Instead, we found a place at the back of a second open chamber of the cave, little visited by tourists.[37] A stone libation table had been found there, indicating that it too was a sacred place. As was becoming our custom, we placed offerings, jewelry, and the little image of the Neolithic goddess, on a large rock that became our altar. After we grounded and centered ourselves, we sang the Mountain Mother song I had received at the Church of the Panagia in Chains. The milk Carol used for her libation had soured, and it set the tone for the ritual that followed. Carol reminded us that women all too often drink sour milk from mothers who are themselves in chains.

Without planning or prompting, our stories came forth. Few of us had uncomplicated relationships with our mothers. Raised to please men and always to put others first, our mothers often placed the needs of the males in the family before the needs of their daughters. Most of our mothers had a hard time appreciating daughters who refused to play by the rules they had learned so well. In different ways, we each longed for support and affirmation we had not received from our mothers. Martha Ann said that her mother almost never praised her, but that when she was dying, she looked her daughter in the eyes and said, "You are a Queen." "Better late than never," Martha Ann said to us, her voice choking with emotion. We understood that she had wanted to say to her mother, "Why couldn't you have told me this all my life?" Jana said that while her mother had always been a great source of love and support in her personal life, she never seemed to listen when Jana, who had struggled to become a professional cellist, played her beloved instrument for her mom. Carol's mother took her bitterness about her own life out on her daughter, and Carol still felt wounded, though her mother had been dead for many years. Others spoke of failing their daughters. Cathleen, overcome with emotion, could not speak.

For some of us the Goddess was the mother we had writ large, for others, the mother we never had, but for most of us, a combination of the two. For all of us, acknowledging the complexities of our relationships with our mothers, the joy and the pain, the darkness and the light, was an integral part of our pilgrimage to the Goddess.

Amazing Grace

After lunch, we hiked to the smaller, more intimate Trapeza Cave. Recently associated with Kronos, the murderous father of Zeus, it provided a home for the early settlers in Crete during the Neolithic period, and later housed the dead. It has two small, easily accessible, dry, and not claustrophobic rooms. We choose the smaller, darker, round one for our ritual. It could just hold us all, sitting in a circle. Each of us placed her candle on or near a stone we chose for our altar, I added the Neolithic Goddess, and we poured libations. Robin asked if we would join her in singing a modified version of the traditional Protestant hymn, "Amazing Grace," which went like this:

> Amazing grace, how sweet the sound,
> that saved someone like me.
> I once was lost, but now am found,
> was blind, but now I see.

'Twas grace that brought my heart to heal,
And grace my fears released.
'Twas grace that brought me back to Thee,
and grace I still receive.

Through many dangers, storms, and scares,
I have already come.
'Twas grace that brought me safe this far,
and grace will lead me home.

When we've been here ten thousand years,
bright shining as the sun,
in endless days, we'll sing out praise,
as when we first begun.

"Amazing Grace" affirmed the message I was receiving over and over, in many different ways, on the pilgrimage. Yes, my own hard work was a part of what brought me and the group together on this day. But beyond that, there was so much that I had not created, and that was beyond my control—including all the beauty of the universe and love freely given. This was the "amazing grace" I celebrated as I joined Robin in song in the Trapeza Cave.

When we finished singing, Marian said, with tears in her eyes, that the phrase, "for ten thousand years," in what for her was a familiar hymn, took on concrete meaning for the first time. We were sitting in a cave where others sat nearly ten thousand years ago, returning to a vision of the Goddess that was much older than ten thousand years. She suggested we continue the ritual by naming our mother line, ending with "and I am proud." Though I had participated in this ritual before, it took on new meaning in the cave. As I said the words, "I am Carol, daughter of Janet, daughter of Lena, daughter of Dora, and I am proud," it felt as if my connection to the ancestors went all the way back to the beginning.

But these ancestors were not enough—many other women had nurtured us. Someone suggested that we call out all the names of the women friends and mentors who had influenced our lives. The names began to ring off the walls of the cave: Judith, Naomi, Mara, Jude, Jane Ellen Harrison, Marija Gimbutas, Matilda Joslyn Gage, Mary Daly, Adrienne Rich, Ellen, Chris, River, Pat, Rena, Sonia, Ellie, Nena, Maria, Melpo, Charis. Soon we were all shouting names at the same time.

After acknowledging sour milk in the morning, we could affirm amazing grace in the afternoon. The ancestors were with us.

I Once Was Lost

The next morning we visited the small church of the Panagia Kera at Kritsa, nestled in the mountains above Agios Nikolaos. One of its aisles is dedicated Saint Anne, the mother of the Virgin Mary. Its fourteenth century frescoes depict the conception and early life of the Virgin Mary, as told in "The Gospel of James," an apocryphal writing not included in the Bible. Unusually, Saint Anne is portrayed blessing the world from the apse, and the frescoes appear to tell the story from a woman's point of view. Anne looks toward the angel who tells her she will bear a child in her old age, while her husband, who is spending forty days in the wilderness, looks away. The birth of Mary is celebrated in an image of Anne lying on the bed where she has just given birth, while her daughter is being placed in a cot. In another set of panels, Joseph brings a pregnant Mary to the Hebrew priests, but even after she passes the test of drinking

bitter waters, he refuses to believe in her innocence. The stories of Anne and Mary echo the stories of Demeter and Persephone, but in the end there is no joyous reunion between
them. The last panel portrays Mary with Jesus over a "closed
gate," the symbol of her perpetual virginity.

In the other aisle of the church, a crowned woman
wearing a pearl-covered gown feeds a large snake from a
small bowl. Identified as Mother Earth, her connection to
the snake is reminiscent of the Snake Goddesses of a much
earlier time. On the opposite wall, a companion fresco depicts Mother Sea as a mermaid. How did such images find
their way onto the walls of a church? Could it be that all was
not forgotten? Closer inspection reveals the subject matter
of these frescoes as the Last Judgment. An unseen God is calling on Mother Earth and Mother Sea to return the bodies of
the dead to Him. Coffins have been opened, and vultures
and fish are coughing up the bodies they have eaten. The
Mothers accept everyone, but God the Father will choose
among them, consigning some to heaven, and condemning
others to the eternal fires of hell.

So much has been lost.

Back on the bus, one of the women asked me to explain why I kept saying that North Americans could learn
an important lesson from the Greeks who throw up their
hands and say, "What can I do?" I answered that Americans tend to believe that we can control everything, that

every problem has a solution, that if we work hard enough, we will get ahead, and that if we try hard enough we will succeed. We tend to think that we should be working all the time, and that when we aren't working, we are slacking off. We don't allow ourselves time to enjoy the simple pleasures of life. When things don't go as we had planned, we blame ourselves. We keep trying harder. It is a vicious cycle.

Living in Greece, I continued, I have learned that everyone does not think as we do. The Greeks work hard, but they also find time to enjoy life. They do not believe that any individual can control everything. This is why they so often throw up their hands and say, "What can I do." This cultural style can lead to fatalism or failure to take responsibility. On the other hand, it expresses a truth we often fail to recognize. There are many things that are not under anyone's control. Wisdom is knowing what we can change and what we cannot, and not expecting everything can be as we want it to be.

I coughed and paused before continuing. I learned this lesson in a general way when I first came to Greece, I said, but in my new therapy group, I discovered that deep down I still believe that I must control everything or the world will fall apart. You have seen this on the pilgrimage. Did you notice how angry I got when the guard at Mount Juctas failed to show up? Would the pilgrimage have been ruined if we had not gone to Mount Juctas? Did the world come to an end when we were unable to visit the Eilitheia Cave?

I paused again, my voice faltering. On an even more personal level, I have shared with some of you that I used to think that if I could not find my true love, it must be my fault. If only I did the right therapy, or the right magic spell, or quit my job, or moved to Greece, I could get what I wanted. But what if it is not that simple? What if some things really are not under our control? What if chance and timing play a role? I paused again. I used to think that if I could not find my true love, I might as well die. Now that I have stopped trying so hard to get what I don't have, I am beginning to recognize what I do have. Love is everywhere. We don't have to do anything. We just have to open our eyes. Love might not come in the form of the true love I was seeking, but it is love nonetheless. This is the "amazing grace" we sang about yesterday, and this is what the ancient Cretans celebrated as "the grace of life." By this point, my voice had faded to a whisper. I was thankful to see that the bus was about to turn onto the road to our next stop on our pilgrimage, the archaeological site of Gournia, because I could not have spoken another word.

But Now I'm Found

*G*ournia, a village of ancient Crete built near the bay of Mirabello, was once an important port for trade. The village was excavated by the American archaeologist, Harriet Boyd Hawes, at the beginning of the twentieth century. There is little to distinguish the narrow streets and closely grouped houses of those ancient times from the traditional villages of contemporary Crete.

Because I could not speak, the others read from the guidebook, while I pointed to the various architectural features it discussed. As we walked up the hill passing by limestone thresholds and rooms with staircases leading to floors above, we began to feel what it might have been like to live in a village in ancient Crete.

Arriving at the top of the hill, where there is a small version of a Sacred Center, the group dismissed the idea that a large altar stone was used for the sacrifice of a bull. Someone was pouring water on it. Learning that there was a Kernos Stone with thirty-two carved indentations nearby, the group started looking for a round stone like the one we had seen at Malia, with no success. Finally, Cathleen followed the instructions in the guidebook, and called us to a small rectangular stone about two feet wide, three feet long, and two feet high. Though the indentations in the stone are barely visible, Sue was running her hand over stone, counting them, and soon announced that indeed there were thirty-two. Nuts, seeds, fruit, and Christina's golden raisins emerged from pockets and were placed on the stone. Robin led us in song.

As the energy was waning, Jana stepped forward to say, "Karolina is giving us so much. I want her to know she is loved. I love her." Oh come on now, I thought, I just said that I know I am loved. But with no voice, I could not protest. Robin stepped forward. "I am a priestess," she said, "I join your souls together." Jana stood on tiptoes and gave me a hug. A little over a year later, Jana and I would be making plans to lead tours to Crete together.[38]

Later in the day, we were all swimming in the clear blue sea. "You know," I said, "if you dip three times under the sea you can renew your virginity." "Who wants that?" Patricia asked skeptically. "It is an ancient custom," I explained. The Goddess Hera renewed her virginity with a bath in the sea. It was not literal virginity, but something like vitality and hope." "I'll take that," Patricia said, diving under a wave. I followed.

Exhaustion

$\mathcal{T}$he next day we drove through the wild tropical landscape of eastern Crete to the Sacred Center of Kato Zakros. From Ano or Upper, Zakros, we would hike part way down the Gorge of the Dead, where bones had been deposited in small caves high up on the cliffs. I had only walked through the gorge once, and the trail was not marked. Relinquishing my role as leader, I let the others find the way. It was a hot day, and we were all tired when we arrived in Kato, or Lower, Zakros.

Some were eager to explore the Sacred Center right then, but I didn't have the energy. Leaving them at the entrance to the site, Jana and I repaired to the first of the several small tavernas lining the beach. With a cold beer to moisten my throat, I realized how much I needed to speak about why I was feeling so tired. The words came tumbling out. I told Jana how I had broken down in therapy group the night before the tour, cried myself to sleep, and missed the plane that was to have brought me to Crete. "I have an article my therapist wrote," I continued. "She says that part of the healing process is losing control, as you give up fixed beliefs that no longer serve you. I have been changing my beliefs over the summer," I said tentatively. "I hope I don't have to break down too," Jana said, looking out to sea. "I know what you mean about control," she continued. "When I play the cello in a quartet or an orchestra, I feel that I have to get every note right. I live my life that way too. Sometimes I feel so exhausted, I wonder if I should stop playing the cello." "Maybe you could take a break from playing," I suggested. "I have just come through a three-year period where I wrote almost nothing. Since the night I expressed my anger at Aphrodite, writing has been pouring out of me. A rest could be good." "Maybe so," Jana responded, with an intense look in her eyes, "but I would be afraid to do that." "I'm scared of breaking down," I said. "Do you think I will have to?" "Probably so," Jana replied, "but maybe it won't be as bad as you think it will be."

Our conversation was interrupted by Giannis and Cathleen. It was probably just as well, because we had already said what we needed to say. Our mood changed immediately. I noticed that we were sitting in front of a larger than life size image of the Snake Goddess, painted on the wall. The artist was the dark-haired skinny man sitting under the painting. "Did you have a feeling for the Goddess when you painted that?" I asked him in Greek. "Not really," he said in a tone of utter distain. "They asked me to paint it, and I did. That's all." "That dude really has an attitude," Cathleen said after I translated for her and Jana. "Cathleen, sometimes you really do have a way with words," I said smiling. "A dude with a 'tude," she repeated. "I think I'll call his friend John Revolta." Jana and I burst into uncontrollable laughter. All through lunch, which took a long time coming, we giggled about the dude with a 'tude, who pranced around the restaurant in short cutoffs, helping his alter ego, John Revolta. "That dude is not Greek," Cathleen observed. "He is a long way from home."

After lunch Giannis went to the bus to take the nap I desperately needed. Jana and I changed into our suits for a swim in the crystal turquoise sea. Though the water was cool and refreshing, I was even more tired when we emerged. I wanted to sleep, but I had agreed to go back to the archaeological site with some of the women.

The Dance Is About to Begin

$\mathcal{E}$ ntering the archaeological site of Kato Zakros, which includes a Sacred Center and part of a town on a small hill above it, I felt too tired to continue with the others. As we passed a stone bench to the north and west of the open court, I lay down and closed my eyes. I don't know if I actually slept, but when I opened my eyes, I was in a trance.

I could see the air vibrating, and as I looked up the hill, I could almost see women walking up and down the stepped paths. My eyes were fixed on the path where women I could not quite see with my eyes went about their daily tasks. After a while Cathleen joined me. "I don't want to talk," I said, "but if you sit quietly beside me, you will see women walking in the village. She sat down and said nothing, but smiled broadly and nodded when I asked her if she could see what I saw.

After a while, I moved and sat facing the Central Court. I could still see the vibrations of the air, and as I looked across the

*court, I felt a sense of anticipation. "The dance is about to begin,"
I told Cathleen when she joined me a few minutes later. She nodded. It was an hour before sunset, and the ancient stones were
bathed in the last light of day. Jana and Patricia were talking in
the central shrine room, while the others leaned over the ancient
cistern watching turtles and turtle babies dive into the water and
emerge again. "The dance is about to begin," I said again.*

*Cathleen exclaimed, "I see the path of the dance rising up in
the court. It looks like the Processional Paths we saw at Knossos,
Phaistos, and Malia. Do you see it?" Though I did not "see" it, I
was moved to the court, where I could "feel" it. I raised my arms,
bent at the elbows, and slowly wove my way back and forth across
the court, following a snakelike path I could feel with my feet. As
I neared the center of the court, I almost lost my footing. Turning
to face Cathleen, I gazed at her solemnly, sending energy through
my palms. Cathleen raised her arms in greeting. I turned again,
continuing to trace the snakelike path, back and forth, across the
court. When I reached the south end of the court, I turned again
to greet Cathleen and Robin who was sitting next to her. "The
path you followed was exactly the path I saw," Cathleen cried out
with astonishment. "You were meant to stop at the center." "It was
an ancient path," I said solemnly.*

*Jana and Patricia, who must have been watching, entered
from the northwest entrance to the court. Jana was leading, arms
upraised, tracing another path, walking with the same slow
rhythm in which I had been led. I turned and slowly walked to-*

wards Jana until I could sense the energy flowing between our palms, then we softly touched our upraised hands. Carol, Patricia, Cathleen, and Robin formed a circle around us, and stood, arms upraised one in each of the four directions. Sensing that we were meant to share the blessing with the others, Jana and I turned, walking slowly towards the women standing in the north and south, feeling the energy, then touching their palms. Back to the center, we turned to the east and the west, completing the ceremony. As we turned to face each other again, I whispered to Jana, "We were called to this dance. It was an initiation."

Difficult Passage

Our next destination was Kato Symi, where a guard would be meeting us at the small mountain town's only taverna. The road was narrow and our bus was large, the curves in the road torturous. I was worried because the guard had warned me that the bus would not be able to traverse the six-kilometer stone and dirt road from the village to the archaeological site. I urged the group to pray that the bus could take us there. I hated to think of coming such a long way, only to be forced to turn back.

When we reached Kato Symi the bus could barely navigate the tree-lined streets of the village. The guard, a small, gruff man with a big mustache, immediately informed our driver that the bus could go no farther. I was distraught. Some of the women were upset and afraid. We decided to park the bus and retreat to the taverna to discuss our options. Our nerves were soothed by the sound of running water,

CAROL P. CHRIST

flowing down in channels from the cold spring that emerges near the site of the ancient temple.

While I attempted to calm the group, not feeling particularly calm myself, Giannis and the guard found a solution. Two pudgy brothers, each with his own farm truck, were having lunch in the taverna. They would take us to the site and bring us back. While Giannis and I were negotiating a price with the brothers, I noticed that the food on their plates looked really good. "Do you think we could eat here?" I asked Giannis. "Why not?" he replied. A few minutes later, the owner of the taverna pulled half of a freshly slaughtered lamb out of the refrigerator, promising that his wife would cook it into a stew while we were gone. All problems resolved, we piled into the farm trucks and set off.

The archaeological site at Kato Symi is high in the mountains, but not on their peak. Even higher mountains surround it, a spring gives birth to flowing stream, a cave opens on the sheer rock face above, and the turquoise sea is visible far below. The site had a continuity of worship for two millennia. First to be worshipped here was the Mountain Mother, then she gained a Son, and finally they were transformed into Aphrodite and Hermes of the Tree. An ancient plane tree, its trunk scarred by fire, is a reminder not only of Hermes of the Tree, but also of the Holy Mother Tree of an earlier era.

The plane tree was the perfect place for a ritual dedicated to Sappho and Aphrodite. Sappho, who lived in the sixth century B.C.E., centuries after the end of the culture of ancient Crete, was known as the greatest of the lyric poets and "the tenth muse" in the classical Greek period. Several of her poems were dedicated to Aphrodite, and her focus on the sensual beauty of the passing moment evokes the grace of life celebrated in ancient Crete. Reading her poems on our pilgrimage would affirm the creative power of women through the ages, including our own.

While some of us explored the site, others created an altar on a thick plank supported by stones that had been wedged into the open cavity of the tree's trunk that had been created many years ago by a fire. I added the familiar Neolithic Goddess to the gifts already on the altar, and removed my necklace, draping it over the Goddess. Soon milk and honey, water and wine, flowed on the altar and into the ground. Once again, Robin led us in song.[39]

Though she had never visited Crete, in one of her poems to Aphrodite, Sappho seemed to be describing the very place where we were standing.

> You know the place
> . . .
> waiting where the grove is
> pleasantest, by precincts

sacred to you, incense
smokes on the altar, cold
streams murmur through the

apple branches . . .

Patricia, who had fallen in love with the sheep and goats dotting the hillsides throughout our journey, and who was mother of two lovely daughters she doted upon, found these words:

You are the herdsman of evening

Hesperus, you herd
homeward whatever
Dawn's light has dispersed

You herd sheep—herd
goats—herd children
home to their mothers.

Jana, ever a sensualist, read:

I confess

I love that
which caresses
me.

"Others have criticized that part of me," Jana added. "But I affirm it." I gave thanks for the grace inspires me to write:

It is the Muses

Who have caused me
to be honored: they

taught me their craft.[40]

In a way that seemed almost uncanny, each woman found a poem that seemed to have been written just for her. The ritual complete, we poured a final libation for Sappho and the Muses, for Aphrodite, and for the Mountain Mother.

Back at the taverna, while we were enjoying yet another perfect meal, our host Manolis, a tall, graceful, grey-haired gentle man, took out his violin and began to play Cretan music for us. When he finished, Karen asked if she could play his instrument. What followed was a European violin solo so sad and so joyful, so hauntingly beautiful, that it seemed we had entered into a dream.

Giveaway

*T*he Idean Cave in the Psiloritis mountains was the last destination on our pilgrimage. Our bus climbed up and up again, passing above a deep gorge and eventually turning left at the village of Anogeia and continuing to climb. From there on, the smooth grey marl bedrock of Crete was exposed. Sheep and goats crossed the road and blended back into the landscape. An occasional vulture circled overhead.

The Idean Cave is on the tallest mountain in Crete, situated on the other side of the same range where we had seen the Kamares Cave from Phaistos. It, like the Dictean Cave we had visited a few days earlier, was said to have been the birthplace of the baby Zeus. But by now the group had learned that, like all of the caves in Crete, the Idean Cave would originally have been sacred to the Mountain Mother. The cave is twenty-one kilometers outside of Anogeia, where we would spend the night. Just below the cave, the Nidan Plateau, green and dotted with hundreds of sheep, came into view. When we got out of the bus, we were greeted by the music of their bells.

It was cold on Mt. Ida, and we pulled our sweaters from our bags. The thirty minute hike up the mountain calmed our ever-active minds and invigorated our bodies. Jana and I were the first to reach the cave. "This is more of a cavern than a cave," Jana remarked, as her eyes took in the enormous mouth and travelled down to what, in comparison with the other caves we had visited, was a wide open space below. A staircase built of wide planks by the archaeologists, made the descent easy. The bird droppings on the wooden platform at the bottom of the cave reminded us that for the ancient Cretans, the appearance of birds during a ritual was considered to be the appearance of the Goddess. "No problem with that here," Jana remarked.

While waiting for the others, we found a dark place in the back of the cave and a freestanding rock that looked like a miniature mountain to use as the altar.[41] Everyone had a copy of the Neolithic Goddess we now called the "Tour Goddess," provided by Giannis, who had made a special trip to the shop at Knossos to purchase them for the group. We found homes for each and every one of them on the rock altar and added our candles. We had created a village with our little Goddesses, and now that they were many, rather than one, the Goddesses reflected each of us.

After pouring libations, sweet and sour, to the Mountain Mother, and singing to her, we placed the gifts we had brought for a final Giveaway ritual near the altar. The Giveaway ritual is known to us as a Native American tradition, but in fact it is a legacy of many pre-patriarchal cultures, and is echoed in the Cretan custom of generosity we had experienced many times on our journey. Each of us in turn closed her eyes, and without looking, chose a gift. Jana received Patricia's offering, and then Patricia received Jana's, a synchronicity that appropriately marked their growing friendship. I gave a blue protective eye, and received a tiny seal stone. When I looked at it in the light I saw that it pictured a couple in the position Mr. Nikos had been too polite to describe when he spoke of a similar image found in the Skoteino Cave.

All gifts given and received, Carol wove us together with red yarn. As we repeated the words, "We say goodbye" three times, we broke the cords that bound us to the others. On the way down the mountain, some of us tied pieces of red yarn to a tree, while others took them home. Just before we reached the Nidan Plain, a flock of sheep crossed in front of us, creating a final concert with their bells.

Mountain Women

When we arrived in Anogeia, Aristeia, the owner of the small hotel where we would spend the night, and her sister Constantina were waiting for us. Captivated by their vivacity and strength when I met them in the spring, I asked Aristeia if they would be willing to share their stories with the group. "Why are you so late?" Constantina began, as soon as I got off the bus. "I'm sick, and I should be in bed, but I'm here as a favor to you," she chided. I hadn't expected them to be waiting, but I hastily apologized. "We'll start as soon as the group puts their bags in the rooms."

As soon as most of us were seated in chairs on Aristeia's front porch, Constantina, a small, round, white-haired woman in her seventies, began to speak rapidly in Cretan dialect, her short arms flailing, her legs swinging back and forth, not quite touching the ground. Our evening sharing stories began as a free-for-all. I tried to stop Constantina long enough to translate, and was forced to shout in English over her Greek. Giannis helped me with words I did not understand. Noticing the rapport that had developed between us, Constantina interrupted her story to ask Giannis in Cretan if he was "banging" me. "Absolutely not," he replied. "For Karolina, I have the greatest respect." Satisfied, she picked up where she had left off.

Constantina's story was hair-raising, fully worthy of the high drama she created. She is thirteen years older than her sister Aristeia. Though Aristeia went to school and learned to read, when Constantina was little, they told her that the teacher hit the children, and sent her into the mountains with the sheep. Her marriage was arranged during the war— she had not been in love with her husband. "And sex?" someone interjected. "Once a year was enough for me," she said, making the rude gesture of slapping her fist against her hand.

When the Germans evacuated Anogeia in response to resistance activities, she was eight months pregnant with her first child. She and three hundred other pregnant women were marched down the mountains to another village where they were held in captivity. One night she heard voice calling her name. A friend of a relative had come to rescue her. Wine had been given to the German guards who got drunk and passed out. Constantina and her savior escaped through the mountains. When they reached Anogeia, they saw that the whole village had been burned to the ground. Constantina wanted to go to her house to see if she could salvage anything. A young German soldier, who knew her, stopped her, telling her that anyone found in the village would be shot. "Why did the German help you?" someone interjected. "Not all the fingers on your hand are the same," Constantina responded. He was a good boy who had been drafted." Constantina and the man who saved her continued on through the mountains looking for word of Constantina's husband. In one village, the men were in the streets playing the lyra and singing. Constantina said, "Have you no shame? Don't you know that Anogeia has been burned?" "That is why we are singing," the men replied. "What else can we do?" In that village or the next one, Constantina learned that her husband was alive. "The war was difficult," she concluded. "We had nothing. Most of our young men were killed."

There was a lull in the conversation, and Aristeia, a strong wiry woman with curly grey hair pulled back tightly in a bun, stepped in. "I am so glad you are all here," she began. "I was so happy to meet Karolina in the spring. Life in the villages is hard for women. I think all women should be feminists. If we ran the world, things would be different. We need to get more women into politics. I'd like to know what all of you are doing about that."

We went around the circle, with each woman sharing a little about her life and work. Many of the women were married and feminists. This surprised Constantina. But not as much as the response Robin gave her when she asked her if she had a boyfriend. "I don't think she wants one," the young Greek school teacher who had joined us, translated diplomatically. "Why not?" Constantina insisted. She got her answer. I don't think Constantina had ever heard the word "lesbian." "Two women together?" she kept repeating. "Why not?" Aristeia responded. Constantina shook her head, trying to figure out how to fit one open palm into the other. As the women shared their stories, Aristeia interjected, "Good, good!" "Bravo, bravo!" She told us that her husband had been out with the sheep while she delivered and then raised her children alone. The only time he was home for any length of time was after he got sick. "When he died," she continued, "I started with rooms-to-rent, and then built this hotel with money I made and a loan from the bank. My daughters said, 'Name this hotel after yourself. You did all the work.' So I did."

Experience had made Aristeia and Constantina hard as rock. Like Mount Ida, they would endure. They were images of the Goddess we sought, reflecting the strength we were discovering within ourselves.

Sisterhood

$\mathcal{E}$ ver since being called to the dance at the Sacred Center of Kato Zakros, Jana, Robin, Patricia, Cathleen, and I had gravitated to each other. On our last afternoon in Heraklion, we found ourselves together again at lunch. Some of the group had stopped to buy postcards, others went shopping. Robin looked around the table and commented, "Isn't it amazing that we have been drawn together?" We looked around the table. On the surface, we were an unlikely combination. Cathleen and Robin often got on each other's nerves. On another day, Patricia would be demurely dressed, attending parties in Washington high society with her husband. Cathleen would always be loud and uncontrollable. Robin was a softer free spirit. Jana lived a quiet life in rural Virginia. I had an exotic one in Athens. But something had called us to each other.

We began talking about the dance in Zakros. We called it an "initiation," but could not articulate its meaning. The Goddess had not appeared in the midst of the dance, but we sensed that She had guided our steps. "We must keep in touch by letter," we agreed, "so that we remember." We spent the afternoon shopping for a symbol of the mystery to spark our memories. When we found it, we promised that we would never tell anyone its meaning.

We hurried back to the hotel to catch the bus that would take us to the ferryboat. Giannis gave me a large round cookie tin filled with the tiny olives found only in Crete as we said good-bye. Before the tour began, our travel agent Rena told me that a driver could make or break a trip. Among the many blessings I had received on the pilgrimage, I counted Giannis. Watching the group ascend the stairs of the ferryboat, I was deeply moved. Though we would have one more day together in Athens, this was the end of our pilgrimage in Crete.

Part Four

REBIRTH

I approached the gates of death,
and set foot on Proserpine's threshold,
yet was permitted to return.[42]

Incubation

*A*fter saying good-bye to the group on our last night in Athens, I went home and collapsed. For several weeks, I spent almost every day in bed, watching television, sleeping, and coughing whenever I tried to speak. Though I was ill, I did not feel the familiar sadness and depression. The pilgrimage had gone better than I had ever dared hope. But I was too tired to think about what it had meant for me. I needed to rest. I gave myself permission to do nothing. In fact, I didn't have much choice. It was a struggle to drag myself out of bed, and talking on the phone brought on coughing fits.

Much of the next two weeks feels hazy in my mind. I must have been in the midst of the "breakdown" I told Jana I feared. According to Charis, as old meaning systems stop functioning, and with no new systems in place, a person will feel at a loss, adrift, unsure of herself and others.[43] Melpo had been feeling this way too. We spoke several times a day, reassuring each other.

I got out of bed after six days to meet with the therapy group. Charis was not there. Patrick smiled encouragingly as I spoke. "The tour went really well," I began. "Everyone loved it. The only problem was that I was extremely tired during the whole trip, and I am exhausted now. I couldn't stop crying after therapy three weeks ago, and because of that, I missed my plane, and then another night's sleep. I was afraid I would not be able to regain control in order to lead the group. I'm afraid of losing control, because I feel like I have two personalities. The one that is sad, is so sad, she wants to commit suicide. I am afraid of her."

"The timing may have been bad," Patrick said, removing his glasses and looking directly into my eyes, "but I'm glad you lost control. You may be scared, but I like the person who is here now. She is not trying so hard. She feels softer and less driven than the Karolina we knew. She is human and vulnerable. I think she is the real you. Everybody likes her." He hesitated, put his glasses back on, and smiled shyly, clearly aware that I was skeptical. "Everyone likes her," he repeated with great kindness. "Look and see." I looked around the circle of women and saw everyone smiling at me. "I want to hug you," one of the women said, getting up and crossing the room to put her arms around me.

I wasn't sure what to make of Patrick's words, but I took comfort in his calm, accepting manner. "It didn't really matter to the others that I was tired on the trip," I added. "No one expected me to be in control of everything. The group seemed to enjoy discovering Crete together. People kept appearing to help me, even when I didn't think I needed help. I didn't have to do everything myself."

When I got home, I went back to bed, but I wasn't afraid any more. Something was changing inside of me. I felt like a snake hibernating in a hole in the ground or a butterfly transforming in a cocoon. Gradually, I came to understand that the timing of my breakdown was exactly right. In many spiritual traditions it is understood that a person must become ill in order to receive transforming insight. The stronger the will, the harder it is to let go. My control had to be taken from me.

Beginnings

"*I*t sounds to me like you are 'sick and tired,'" Rena said when she called. "'Sick and tired of it all,'" she repeated definitively. Her words felt exactly right, and hearing them spoken aloud made me wonder why I felt that way. It began to dawn on me that I was sick and tired of the constant struggle to stay in control. As I lay in my bed, drifting in and out of sleep, I heard my father's words: "Control yourself." He would say it when I was crying, when I was angry, and even when my brother and I were just having fun. It was not only sadness and anger that I had learned to control, but joy as well.

One of the times my father told me to "control myself" was when my brother was born. My mother and my baby brother were in the back seat of the car, my father was driving, and I was standing up and turning around in the front seat in order to see the baby. I can still see myself in a newly starched dress and little white shoes jumping up and down in excitement. "Control yourself," my father said. "You are a big girl now." I was all of two-and-one-half years old.

As I had studied psychology, I wondered if my brother's birth had been traumatic for me. I imagined that I might have been insanely jealous of my baby brother. What I now remembered was joy. Of course children are jealous of new babies. They need to be reassured that they are still loved. But my mother was busy with a demanding baby, and my father did not tell me what I needed to hear. In my mind, I must have felt that the only way I could retain my parents' love was by "controlling myself" and becoming "a big girl." It was too hard. I was only a little girl. But I tried. And I had been trying ever since.

Alice Miller eloquently describes the situation of children raised with the poisonous pedagogy of control who learn that they can gain their parents' love only if they please them. Deprived of spontaneous affection and love, they come to regard the world as a dangerous place that can only be maneuvered by those who maintain control. Yet love gained through self-control and control of others can never be sure and sustaining. Not allowed to experience joy in simply living and breathing, these children grow up lonely, unhappy, and depressed.[44] One of these children, I had been suffering depression off and on all my life.

I began to understand that the voice that says, *"No one understands me, no one loves me, I might as well die,"* was born in the struggle to suppress my feelings, to grow up, to control myself. Little Carol had never really wanted to die. All she had ever wanted was love. What she needed to say was: *"I hurt, I want, I feel, I am."*

Now when I hear the words, *"No one loves me, no one understands me, I might as well die,"* echoing in my mind again—and I will hear them from time to time—I will not be so afraid. I will feel sympathy for little Carol and for big Carol, for whom the struggle to stay in control was just too difficult. I will replace the refrain of ancient pain with the words they masked: *"I hurt. I feel. I want. I am."* The darkness I feared did not hold a monster. It held human feeling.

A Serpentine Path

" *I* n the next days, I rested and my cough got better. I
felt soft, open, and as vulnerable as a newborn baby.
I spoke often with Melpo, and I received letters and photographs from Jana and Patricia. As I wrote back, memories of
Zakros became vivid. Thinking of the snakelike path I had
traced on the ancient stones, my eyes fixed on the gold snake
bracelet on my right arm. I reviewed the many meanings the
symbol of the snake held in ancient cultures. Goddess temples were used for storing grain, the harvest returned to She
who presided over it. Snakes were guardians of the temples,
eating the mice and rats that came to take the grain. The
coiled snake and the snake biting its tail are symbols of
wholeness. Snakes shedding their skins are images of rebirth
and regeneration. Snakes hibernate under the earth and are
reborn. But there was more: the rhythm of the snake in
movement. I picked up a pen and wrote: *"a serpentine path."*

These words described our initiation in the dance at Zakros: the serpentine path is the path of life, a snakelike, meandering path, winding in and out, up and down, with no beginning and no end, into the darkness, into the light.[45] There is no goal, only the journey.

A cycle was coming to completion in my life. Through hard work and amazing grace, I found my way back to the Goddess, to myself. The mystery that was revealed to me as my mother died was unfolding in my life. Love had never abandoned me and never would. The Goddess would be with me at every turn in the path, and in that knowledge. I could give up control and open myself to life.

And I wanted to live! I could trust myself and my intuition because I was no longer confused by fear and desire. The Muse had come back to me, words were flowing. I would return again and again to the mountains and caves of Crete, by myself, with friends, and with other pilgrims. My life would be filled with grace abounding and love overflowing.

I felt the sense of anticipation that came over me at Kato Zakros. The dance is about to begin: the dance of my life. It begins anew every day.

Epilogue

The mystery I learned in Crete did indeed change my life, both immediately and in the long term. On the second pilgrimage, while we were enjoying another of her delicious meals, Christina told me that when she lights candles for her family, she always lights one for me. Her words had the force of revelation: I would never again hear the words *"no one loves me"* in my mind. During one of the following tours, in silent meditation in the Skoteino Cave, I realized that I was no longer asking the Goddess for what I thought I wanted, or even for guidance. I was simply sitting in the darkness with my eyes open, listening to water dripping in the cave. And that was enough.

Some might ask whether my healing was spiritual or psychological. Surely there were elements of both. My insights occurred in spaces that were overtly sacred, with other people, and in therapy. Our modern culture has separated psychology—whose root is *psyche* or soul—from spirituality, and we also tend to separate self from others. These distinctions were not known in earlier cultures: healing was in the hands of wise women and shamans and "medicine" included herbal remedies, human intervention, and prayer. Although I—and the reader along with me—can separate moments in my healing, for me, there was one journey in which I found the lost parts of myself and wove them into a new whole.

I have now led forty Goddess Pilgrimages to Crete, with over five hundred women participating in them.[46] Most of these women have returned stronger in themselves and in their convictions that a different world is possible. I am often asked why I continue to lead tours in Crete rather than moving on. My answer is simple: there are not many places in the world where we can experience a genuinely pre-patriarchal civilization with so many sites excavated and so many beautiful artifacts preserved. I choose to deepen my knowledge of a land and a culture I know well, one that continually offers new gifts.

Though I did not move to Crete, it has become my second home. Many of the Cretan people mentioned in this book, and others too, have become like family. Our groups were invited to two village-wide weddings, and I have watched the children of these marriages become teen-agers while their parents' hair turns grey. Mr. Nikos, Manolis the violin player, and other good friends have died, but memories of their kindness and friendship remain in my heart.

When we visit the museums of Crete, I speak with confidence about images that have become familiar to me through many years of study. I become ever more convinced that Marija Gimbutas was right that the spirals, triangles, and other symbols on pitchers and bowls and jars express "the language of the Goddess." New research on egalitarian matriarchal cultures provides grounding for her hypothesis that the cultures of Old Europe, including Crete, were matrifocal, matrilineal, and probably matrilocal. Despite popular misconceptions, matriarchal cultures are not female-dominant. Councils of grandmothers and great-uncles make decisions for the group, taking account of everyone's needs. Both girls and boys are encouraged to become as generous and loving as the grandmothers, mothers, and aunts who nurture them.[47] The matriarchal customs of gift-giving and give-away have persisted in the generous spirit of rural Cretans. That matriarchal values could survive three and a half thousand years of patriarchy and war is, to me, nothing less than miraculous.[48]

Aspects of the path of the pilgrimage have changed, yet much has remained the same. We still visit Paliani, the caves, the mountains, the museums, and the archaeological sites. Christina still feeds us, and Kostas still plays for us. We have added a ritual of naming and pouring libations for the dead—ancestors, relatives, friends, and animal companions. Though we did not walk a labyrinth on the first tour, a few years later, we found a Cretan-style labyrinth in an open field near a traditional threshing floor. We have maintained it ever since.[49] There, we dance in the labyrinth with upraised arms, touching hands as we pass each other, while singing the words, "There is a path to the mystery, and as I walk it's revealed to me."[50]

Not long ago, I reconnected with Ramona and Jassy, a mother and a daughter who came on the Goddess Pilgrimage together. The tour was Jassy's dream—Ramona came to enjoy a vacation in Crete with her daughter. On the last day of the pilgrimage, Ramona wrote me a note saying, "I came expecting nothing, and I received everything." Participating in a ritual for the dead on the third day of the tour, she felt an enormous energy coursing through her body, and she knew at that moment that she had found a spiritual vision that made sense to her. Later, while co-leading the labyrinth ritual, she felt the presence of ancient priestesses. In the ensuing years, Ramona learned to create labyrinths and to share the experience of walking them with others. Jassy, an artist, has not stopped painting "in the language of the Goddess" since she returned home, and is now leading workshops that guide other women to paint images of female power.[51]

The serpentine path continues to unfold.

*Spiraling
into
the center,
and
out again*

Notes

1. See Maureen Murdock, *The Heroine's Journey: Woman's Quest for Wholeness* (Boston: Shambala Press, 2009); and Patricia 'Iolana, *Literature of the Sacred Feminine: Great Mother Archetypes and the Re-Emergence of the Goddess in Western Traditions* (Saarbrucken, Germany: VDM Verglag, 2009).

2. For information on the Goddess Pilgrimage to Crete, see www.goddessariadne.org.

3. Thealogy, from *thea*, Goddess, and *logos*, meaning.

4. Carol P. Christ, "Elie Wiesel's Stories: Still the Dialogue," Yale University dissertation, 1974; *Diving Deep and Surfacing: Women Writers on Spiritual Quest* (Boston: Beacon Press, 1980, 1985, 1995); *Laugher of Aphrodite: Reflections on a Journey to the Goddess* (San Francisco: Harper & Row, 1987).

5. Carol P. Christ, *Rebirth of the Goddess: Finding Meaning in Feminist Spirituality* (New York: Routledge, 1998 [1997]); *She*

Who Changes: Re-imagining the Divine in the World (New York: Palgrave Macmillan, 2003); with Judith Plaskow, *Goddess and God in the World: Conversations in Embodied Theology* (Minneapolis: Fortress Press, 2016).

6. Homer, *The Odyssey*, Book X!, Walter Shewring, trans. (Oxford: Oxford University Press, 1980), 128.

7. *Sappho: A New Translation*, Mary Barnard, trans. (Berkeley, CA: University of California Press, 1958), #63.

8. Vincent Scully, *The Earth, the Temple, and the Gods: Greek Sacred Architecture*, rev. ed. (New Haven: Yale University Press, 1980), 217-219.

9. Not his real name.

10. Jane Ellen Harrison, *Prolegomena to the Study of Greek Religion* (London: Merlin Press, 1962), 274.

11. I Corinthians 13: 1-8a, 13, quoted from the Revised Standard Version of the Bible.

12. Christine Downing, *The Long Journey Home: Revisioning the Myth of Demeter and Persephone for Our Time* (Boston: Shambala Press, 1994). 125-139.

13. Bernard, *Sappho*, #84.

14. The archaeological service has since restored the icon, removing the silver hands, feet, and haloes.

15. Bogdan Rutkowski, *The Cult Places of the Aegean* (New Haven: Yale University Press, 1987), 51/

16. The Homeric Hymn "To Demeter" states that the Eleusinian Mysteries originated in Crete; see Thelma Sargent, trans., *The Homeric Hymns: A Verse Translation* (New York: W.W. Norton, 1973), 5.

17. The water mill is now preserved as a museum.

18. The first Goddess Pilgrimage to Crete was in the fall of 1993.

19. George Sfikas, *Trees and Shrubs of Greece*, Ellen Sutton, trans. (Athens: Efstathiades Group, 1978), 104.

20. Barmard. *Sappho*, #23.

21. Lucy Goodison, *Moving Heaven and Earth: Sexuality, Spirituality, and Social Change* (London: The Women's Press, 1990), 68.

22. Knossos was repaired and reused by the Myceneans.

23. Jacquetta Hawkes, *Dawn of the Gods* (London: Sphere Books, 1972).

24. The museum has since been reorganized.

25. Marija Gimbutas, *The Language of the Goddess* (San Francisco: Harper & Row, 1989).

26. Nanno Marinatos, *Minoan Religion: Ritual, Image, and Symbol* (Columbia, SC: University of South Carolina Press, 1993, 38-75).

27. Since then, trees have blocked the view of Mount Juctas.

28. Rituals are no longer permitted on guarded archaeological sites in Crete. We have replaced them with silent walks, readings, and meditations, and have found other places for rituals.

29. See the illustration facing the title page.

30. See note 27.

31. See note 27.

32. Words from a song I learned in the Women's Spirituality Movement, attributed to Native American tradition.

33. See Jeremiah 44:19.

34. See note 27.

35. Since then, a concrete staircase has been built.

36. This small cave has been roped off, to prevent access.

37. See note 27.

38. In the spring of 1995, Jana and I led our first Goddess Pilgrimage to Crete together, through Ariadne Institute, see note 2.

39. See note 26.

40. Barnard, *Sappho*, # 37, 16, 6, and 98.

41. See note 27.

42. Apuleius, *Transformation of Lucius: Otherwise Known as the Golden Ass*, Robert Graves, trans. (New York: Farrar, Straus & Giroux, 1951), 280

43. Charis Katakis, "Stages of Psychotherapy: Progressive Reconceptualizations as a Self-Organizing Process, *Psychotherapy, Theory, Research, Practice, and Training 26* (1989), 484-93.

44. Alice Miller, *For Your Own Good: Hidden Cruelty in Child-Rearing and the Roots of Violence* (New York: Noonday Press, 1990 [1983]).

45. After the tour, Jana Ruble arranged the repeated words "Light and Darkness" to an old European melody. Symbolizing one of the mysteries we learned on the pilgrimage, we have sung it on every subsequent tour; It has found its way into other sacred settings, including the Christian feminist Re-Claiming Conference.

46. See note 2.

47. Heide Goettner-Abendroth, ed., *Societies of Peace: Matriarchies Past, Present and Future* (Toronto: Inannna Publications, 2009); Peggy Reeves Sanday, *Women at the Center: Life in a Modern Matriarchy* (Ithaca, NY: Cornell University Press, 2002).

48. Carol P. Christ, "Is the Spirit of Great Generosity in Crete a Survival of Ancient Matriarchal Values?" http://feminismandreligion.com/2013/10/28/is-the-spirit-of-great-generosity-in-crete-a-survival-of-ancient-matriarchal-values-by-carol-p-christ/, accessed on September 17, 2015.

49. The labyrinth we walk in Mochlos is the traditional Cretan labyrinth that is pictured on coins from Knossos dated to the Hellenistic period; this labyrinth design is reproduced at the head of the chapters of this book. The entrance to the labyrinth in Mochlos is from the right side, which is congruent with the fact that Cretan circle dances move to the right or counterclockwise.

50. From the song, "There is a Path to the Mystery," by Donna Fontanarose Rabuck.

51. See "Jassy Watson Archives," http://feminismandreligion.com/author/jassy11/, accessed November 14, 2015.

CPSIA information can be obtained
at www.ICGtesting.com
Printed in the USA
FFHW011933261018
49003818-53254FF